KT-527-228

SCOTLAND
FROM ABOVE

PHOTOGRAPHS BY COLIN BAXTER

WITH TEXT BY CHRIS TABRAHAM

LOMOND

EDINBURGH ▪ SCOTLAND

Scotland from Above

Scotland from space looks a mere speck of land on a slightly larger speck off the mighty continent of Europe. From this great distance, Scotland looks no different from its neighbours.

But come closer to the earth, soar like an eagle over that speck, and Scotland reveals its true character – a country of mighty mountain peaks and soft undulating hills, of wide-open spaces and dense urban settlement, of rural idyll and heavy industry, 6000 miles of coastline, the United Kingdom's largest mountain system, 30,000 freshwater lochs, 6600 river systems, 800 islands. For a small country, Scotland packs an awful lot into its 30,000 square miles.

Mountains and high hills are everywhere. Even in the green and fertile Central Lowlands, in the river valleys of the Forth and Clyde, rolling hills are all around – the Campsies, the Ochils and the rest – whilst to south and north loom distant heights. The gently rounded Southern Uplands reach across the land from Berwickshire to Galloway, their heather-carpeted hills impressive and rugged in places, though nowhere truly mountainous; Merrick, at 2765 ft (843 m) the highest, falls just short of qualifying as a Munro.

The Southern Uplands pale into insignificance when compared with the mighty Highland peaks that cover vast swathes of the north. The Grampians, the greatest mountain system in the British Isles, stretch from Ben Lomond, within a marathon run of the centre of Glasgow, eastward to the outskirts of Aberdeen, and northward to Gleann Mòr, 'the Great Glen', the huge cleft that almost slices Scotland into two. Big Ben Nevis towers highest of all, whilst Cairngorm's snowy wastes are a sub-Arctic landscape of awesome beauty. Beyond the Great Glen range even more massifs, as far as Ben Hope, from whose summit one can see the most northerly tip of the British mainland, Dunnet Head.

Scotland has been called the land of the mountain and the flood, and deep waters vie with the dizzy heights for attention in the landscape. Nowhere in Scotland is one more than 40 miles from the sea, for long sinuous lochs penetrate deep into the country's west side and broad firths the east. Inland is a myriad of freshwater lochs, some vast, most mere pools, interplaying with innumerable river systems to drain the land. Scotland will never run short of water.

Then there are the islands, hundreds of them, the majority hugging the heavily indented western seaboard; though whether Skye still counts as an island now that it is permanently attached to the mainland by the new bridge remains a moot point. Most are no size at all, and only a very few are inhabited. The hundred or so islands in the northern archipelagos of Orkney and Shetland are more densely settled, though their combined population amounts to less than that of a town the size of Ayr.

Humans first appeared on this speck of land 10,000 years ago, after the passing of the last Ice Age. We have been scratching at the surface of that land ever since, in our various and varied attempts to make it our home. Our oldest ancestors lived in caves close to the shore before venturing inland. There they cleared scrub and put down roots – literally, for they became farmers as well as hunters and gatherers. In the shadow of those mountains, beside those rivers, and on those islands, they lived and worked and socialised, leaving behind them a legacy of settlements, temples and tombs that still fills us with admiration and awe. Nowhere are these more impressive than on mainland Orkney, where the monuments they erected have recently been designated a World Heritage Site.

Orkney's Stone Age monuments owe as much to the natural stone from which they were built as to the skills of their builders; even as bedrock, the soft red Orkney flagstone looks as though it has been artificially crafted. Look down on any area of Scotland, at almost any building, and you will generally be able to tell roughly where you are, be it Aberdeen, the 'granite city', Glasgow and Dumfries with their rich-red tenements and villas fashioned from Upper Old Red Sandstone, the Southern Uplands with their farmsteadings and dykes formed from grey/black whinstone, or the Western Isles where the crofting townships have been hard-wrought from gnarled boulders of Lewisian gneiss, Britain's oldest rock. Modern man-made materials, such as concrete, glass and steel, may have threatened to take their place, but the ancient grain remains.

Scotland has come a long way since those modest Stone Age beginnings. In later prehistory our Bronze Age and Iron Age ancestors tilled and tamed the soil, and lived in mighty hillforts or sturdy broch towers. In the years after Christ, Roman legionaries came and built the Antonine Wall from Firth of Forth to Firth of Clyde, Imperial Rome's most northerly frontier. In the Middle Ages, Norman settlers built impressive abbeys and formidable castles. This was also the era when most of our present towns were first laid out.

During the agricultural revolution of the eighteenth and early nineteenth centuries, our forebears drained the intractable bogs and marshes and floored the fertile river valleys with patchwork-quilt cornfields. They constructed countless miles of road, dug canals, and dotted the long coastline with harbours and lighthouses. And in the nation's capital, Edinburgh, they broke free of the medieval Old Town, constrained on its rocky spine, and built a splendid and magnificent city – the Georgian New Town.

The industrial age of Queen Victoria's long reign saw the railway arrive, and the little cathedral town of Glasgow mushroom into a mighty metropolis, 'the workshop of Empire'. Towns expanded across the Central Lowlands from Greenock to Dundee, and new ones were built, the most famous being the mill village of New Lanark. Down from the Highlands poured the new workforce, and into the emptied straths and glens moved the cheviot and the stag.

During the twentieth century, heavy industries declined; shipyards, mills, mines and factories closed. New hi-tec industries rose from greenfield sites to take their place. Inner-city slums were flattened and their populations decanted to tower-blocks and bungalows out in the suburbs, or to new towns such as Cumbernauld. In the empty Highland glens massive hydro-electric schemes appeared, whilst forests of conifers sprouted up over the Southern Uplands. Both courted controversy, just as modern windfarms do today. The discovery of North Sea oil in the 1960s saw Aberdeen transmute from 'granite city' to 'oil capital' and Scotland's centre of gravity shifted ever so slightly away from the Central Belt towards the north-east. Today, five million people live in Scotland, over half of them in and around Glasgow.

As we soar like an eagle over this land, we see these works of man laid out before us – the cities, towns and villages, the monuments of times past and time present. We see them set against a landscape of great beauty, mountains and lochs and islands that remain as powerfully impressive as when our remote ancestors first set eyes upon them.

Scotland from space may look like a mere speck on a slightly larger speck off the mighty continent of Europe. But soar like an eagle over that speck and Scotland reveals its true character. It is a wonderful sight.

Edinburgh, the Lothians & Borders

Deep waters and high hills frame Scotland's south-east corner – the Firth of Forth and North Sea to north and east, the Cheviot and Lowther Hills to south and west. Within that frame lies a varied landscape of undulating moorland interspersed with fertile river valleys transporting the Tweed, the Tyne and the rest to the sea.

Beneath the heather-carpeted Lammermuirs, Moorfoots, Pentland and Bathgate Hills lies a hard, unyielding bedrock of shale and greywacke that helps form the Southern Uplands, whilst above in the patchwork-quilt fields in the river valleys waves the ripening corn. In centuries past, this entire south-east corner was called Lothian, and it was a frontier zone between Scotland proper, across the Firth of Forth to the north, and Anglo-Saxon England to the south. The Forth was then a national as well as a natural boundary, which they called 'the Scottish Sea'. But Malcolm II's crushing victory over the English in 1018 at Carham, near Coldstream, effectively set the seal on Scotland's claim to Lothian, and firmly established its south-eastern border on the River Tweed. Berwick-upon-Tweed was then Scotland's chief town and seaport, but the continuing wars with England finally put paid to that in 1482. Into its place stepped Edinburgh.

The Forth Bridge

The beautiful city of Edinburgh, Scotland's capital, dominates the region. Man first gazed upon Arthur's Seat, Edinburgh's 'mountain in the city', 9000 years ago, and Roman legionaries marched by in the first century AD on their way to conquer the Caledonian tribes to the north. Today, Edinburgh is home to half a million souls. In the Middle Ages the inhabitants huddled together on the rocky spine of the Old Town, running east from the castle down the Royal Mile, past the High Kirk of St Giles' to the Palace of Holyroodhouse. Now they are spread out across the plain from Currie to Craighall, from Leith to Liberton, dwellers in a city of contrasts – of ramshackle Old Town and classical New Town, of lively centre and leafy suburbs, the Edinburgh of the refined and the 'Embra' of ordinary folk.

Melrose Abbey, Borders

Pretty market towns play second fiddle to Edinburgh, capitals not of their country but of their county – Linlithgow in West Lothian, with its medieval palace, Dalkeith in Midlothian, with its Georgian palace, and Haddington in East Lothian, dominated by St Mary's, the longest burgh kirk in Scotland. Great abbey churches also dominate three Border towns, Kelso, Jedburgh and Melrose. The fourth great Border abbey, Dryburgh, nestles in its sylvan setting beside the Tweed. Other settlements are more workaday, such as the fishing village of Eyemouth, on the Berwickshire coast, the Border mill towns of Hawick, Galashiels and Selkirk, and the industrial towns of the Lothians.

The Border mills and the mines of Lothian are all gone now, and the fishing industry too has all but disappeared. Farming prospers still and the region's natural beauty and rich history sustain a healthy tourism industry. Lately, new hi-tec industries have made their appearance in Silicon Glen, west of Edinburgh, whilst windfarms have started to sprout up from the Lammermuir Hills to the capital's south and west.

Holyrood Abbey & the Palace of Holyroodhouse, Edinburgh

The imposing Palace of Holyroodhouse, at the foot of Edinburgh's Royal Mile, is the
official residence of the British royal family. The royal standard (the Lion Rampant) flies only when they are in residence.
Holyroodhouse – Caledonia's 'Palace of Versailles' – has been the royal family's official Scottish home since the Reformation
of 1560 saw the demise of their former residence, the Augustinian Abbey of Holyrood; its roofless nave can be
seen on the left. Most of the present complex was built for Charles II in the 1670s.

Edinburgh Castle

Edinburgh's Castle Rock (left) was formed 340 million years ago during a period of volcanic activity within the earth. Today it hosts a mighty
stronghold that has dominated its surroundings for centuries. In ancient times Din Eidyn, the stronghold of Eidyn, was the fortress of Mynyddog
'the Magnificent', king of the local tribe. In the middle ages, it became Scotland's chief royal castle, enduring siege after siege during the long wars
with England. In 1566 it witnessed happier times with the birth there of James VI, who in 1603 united the two warring nations under one crown.
Thereafter, the castle served as a garrison fortress, and many of today's buildings date from those twilight days. They include the monstrous seven-
storey New Barracks, built during the Napoleonic Wars in the 1790s. Sir Walter Scott described it as looking like 'a vulgar cotton mill'.
His contemporary, Lord Cockburn, was heard to exclaim: 'Look on the west side of the castle – and shudder!'

Edinburgh Old Town

The crown-towered High Kirk of St Giles' (centre left) emerges from the shadows as the low winter sun passes
across Edinburgh's Old Town. Somewhere in the darkness below lies the body of John Knox, fiery Protestant preacher and the kirk's
first minister. Beyond, across the High Street, rises the solid mass of the City Chambers, whilst far beneath lies a legacy from
Auld Reekie's murky medieval past, Mary King's Close. All around lofty tenements vie with public buildings for space,
and in the shadows beyond are the glass-roofed Waverley Station and Princes Street Gardens.

Edinburgh – Arthur's Seat & the City from the East

Not many European capitals have a mountain in their midst. Edinburgh has – Arthur's Seat,
created over 300 million years ago during a period of intense vulcanic activity and rising up from Holyrood Park to its
summit 823 ft (251 m) above; a haven of peace surrounded by city bustle. Over its right shoulder nestles the medieval 'Old Town',
whilst the foreground is carpeted with neat 1930s bungalows and post-war medium-rise flats.

Edinburgh – West End

Sir George Gilbert Scott's lofty triple-spired St Mary's Episcopal Cathedral, in Palmerston Place, dominates Edinburgh's
western New Town, disturbing the relaxed rhythm set by the graceful curves and angled squares of the surrounding crescents and streets.
This was where Victorian Edinburghers with money settled, in houses noticeably more elaborate than those of their Georgian predecessors,
their projecting bay windows nicely picked out in the warm winter sun.

Edinburgh – west of the Castle

This area west of Edinburgh Castle looked very different a century ago, when the Caledonian Railway Station and the Union Canal's Port Hopetoun and Port Hamilton sprawled over much of it. Both are history now, and graceful modern buildings of stone and glass tower over Lothian Road; they include Edinburgh's International Conference Centre (the circular building left foreground), banking and insurance offices. The round copper dome of the Usher Hall, Edinburgh's principal concert hall, is visible top left.

The Scottish Parliament, Holyrood, Edinburgh

Upturned boats – or fallen leaves? Seen from the air, either seems possible as the inspiration for Enric Miralles' masterpiece, opened in 2004 to house the Scottish Parliament. Top left is the debating chamber and nudging up to it the committee rooms and ministers' accommodation; bottom right the MSP building. Sandwiched between them, its red pantiled roofs contrasting with the acres of concrete and glass, stands the seventeenth-century Queensberry House, housing among other things the Donald Dewar Reading Room, named in honour of the first First Minister of the new Parliament.

Britannia, & Ocean Terminal, Leith, Edinburgh

The Royal Yacht *Britannia* first rolled down a Clydeside slipway in April 1952, and steamed over a million miles flying the flag for Britain. Following its decommissioning in 1997, *Britannia* was brought to its final berth, Leith, and now serves as a popular visitor attraction alongside the shops, bars and cinemas of Ocean Terminal in the rejuvenated seaport.

Flats, Leith, Edinburgh

Leith, Edinburgh's seaport, still has ships coming and going, but many of the dockside warehouses have either been converted into flats, or been demolished to make way for new 'des-reses' such as these.

Edinburgh – New Town (left) & Blackhall (above)

Graceful Royal Circus (foreground) and the elegant broad streets around, such as Great King Street (centre left) and Heriot Row,
where Robert Louis Stevenson was born in 1850, were built almost 200 years ago on the north-facing slope downhill from the original
Georgian New Town (top right). Much of the pale yellow sandstone came from the quarries at Craigleith, a mile to the west.
In 1905, Craigleith's vast hole in the ground was closed, gradually filled in and eventually covered with houses
built of common brick, like those in Blackhall pictured here.

Royal Terrace, Calton Terrace & Regent Terrace, Edinburgh

In the 1820s Edinburgh's Georgian New Town spread eastward to embrace Calton Hill. The architect William Henry Playfair,
one of the stars of the Scottish Enlightenment, combined architecture and nature to create a majestic residential area for the city's well-to-do.
Regent Gardens, between the converging terraces, was designed for their exclusive use.

The Meadows, Edinburgh

Three hundred years ago this part of Edinburgh was the Burgh Loch. It was drained in the eighteenth century and the Meadows has been used for recreation, including cricket matches, ever since. The buildings of the former Royal Infirmary are to the top right.

Belford Gardens & Belford Avenue, Edinburgh

In the 1920s and 30s, many of Edinburgh's inner-city slums were cleared away and replaced by new housing in the greenbelt, including these neat bungalows in Belford – asking price in those days just £400!

Garden Sculpture outside the Gallery of Modern Art, Edinburgh

Charles Jencks' dramatic *Landform*, gracing the area in front of the National Gallery of Modern Art, in Edinburgh's Belford district, is a wonderful new acquisition, complementing the array of artworks within. The artist's swirling, stepped, grass-topped mounds interplay with three crescent pools.

The Forth Bridges and Firth of Forth

There is nothing in the world to compare with the Forth Rail Bridge, that forest of steel spanning the Queensferry Narrows in the Firth of Forth between Lothian and Fife. Even before its formal opening on 4 March 1890, John Fowler and Benjamin Baker's engineering masterpiece was being hailed as the eighth wonder of the world. The simple statistics are staggering enough: 1.5 miles (2.5 km) long; 340 ft (104 m) high at its highest point; 55,000 tons of steel, 700,000 cu ft (19,822 cu metres) of stone; and 8,000,000 rivets, the last one driven home by the Prince of Wales at the opening ceremony. The Road Bridge, a far sleeker suspension bridge designed by Freeman Fox and Partners, joined it in 1964.

Linlithgow Palace & St Michael's Church, West Lothian

The majestic royal palace of the Stewarts beside Linlithgow Loch today lies roofless and ruined, yet the visitor still feels a sense of
awe on entering its portal. Begun by James I after a fire in 1424 destroyed its predecessor, Linlithgow became an elegant palace, and a welcome
stopping-place for the royal family along the busy road between Stirling and Edinburgh. The proud burgesses of the town, not wishing to be
outshone, rebuilt their town kirk, St Michael's (right). The aluminium 'crown of thorns' atop its west tower was added in 1964. Important events
in the palace included two royal births, those of James V in 1512 and his daughter Mary Queen of Scots in 1542.

The Bass Rock (left) and North Berwick (above), East Lothian

The Bass Rock rises like a giant boulder from the sea. 23,000 gannets live there today, and the entire rock turns to
brilliant white when the sun shines on its carpet of guano. Man, too, has lived there intermittently and reluctantly – as soldiers,
prisoners and lighthouse keepers. But we much prefer the dry land and pretty surroundings of North Berwick.
Visitors can admire the gannets from the award-winning Scottish Seabird Centre beside the harbour.

Horseley Hill, Borders

The familiar Lowland landscape of patchwork-quilt fields,
typified here in the eastern Borders, was created during the agricultural revolution 300 years ago when the
centuries-old tradition of communally farmed, broad open rigs was replaced by enclosures, individually tenanted.
On the horizon is a far more recent revolution – a windfarm on the Lammermuir Hills.

St Abb's Head, Borders

The spectacular 300 ft (91 m) high cliffs at St Abb's Head, on the Berwickshire coast,
were home to St Ebba and her nuns in the seventh century, and from 1862 to the lighthouse keepers. Ever present throughout all
this time have been the large breeding colonies of guillemots, kittiwakes, razorbills, fulmars, shags and puffins; St Abb's Head
National Nature Reserve has been managed by the National Trust for Scotland since 1980.

25

Eildon Hills, Borders

The Romans came, saw and conquered the Borders in the first century AD, and built a great legionary fortress in the shadow of the Eildon Hills, near Melrose. They named their new base Trimontium, after Eildon's three mountains, though the highest point, the central summit, is just 1385 ft (422 m) high. Eildon Hill North (foreground) is encircled by a 3 mile (5 km) long rampart and crowded with the foundations of hundreds of prehistoric roundhouses. Estimates suggest the population would have been a staggering 6000 people, though most appear to have left before the Romans appeared on the distant horizon.

Dryburgh Abbey, Borders

Graceful Dryburgh Abbey, nestling in sylvan seclusion in the heart of the Border country, was founded in 1150 by white-robed Premonstratensian canons from Alnwick, Northumberland. They spent most of their waking day in their abbey church (on the left) and the remainder in and around their rectangular cloister (right). The 'white canons' have been gone these past 400 years, but the beautiful pink sandstone walls continue to offer visitors a peaceful refuge from the outside world. Both Sir Walter Scott (d1832) and Earl Haig (d1928) chose to be buried here.

Glasgow & South-West Scotland

High in the Lowther Hills, midway between Glasgow and the English Border, two great rivers begin their long journeys to the sea – the River Annan south and east to the Solway Firth, the Clyde north and west to the Firth of Clyde. Together they define Scotland's south-west corner.

Great Western Road, Glasgow

The region is one of contrasts. The brown, heather-clad Galloway Hills divide the douce green fields of Dumfriesshire and Ayrshire. The rugged cliff-edged Rinns of Galloway in the far south-west keep apart the yellow slivers of shining sand that fringe the estuaries of Clyde and Solway. In the north the rolling hills of Strathclyde – 'strath' simply means a broad valley – continue to defy the seemingly unending urban sprawl. Nowhere though does that contrast seem greater than in the 40 short miles (60 km) that separate sleepy Wanlockhead, high up in those Lowther Hills and at 1500 ft (450 m) Scotland's highest village, from the '24/7' metropolis of Glasgow, Scotland's largest city.

The rocks underlying the surface define the character of the built landscape, here as elsewhere. The dour, unyielding greywackes (shales), laid down 400 million years ago to form the Southern Uplands of Scotland, are everywhere in farm buildings and field dykes. The softer, younger sandstones, ranging in hue from pale yellow to blood red, were exploited in Victorian times to create the great city of Glasgow and the industrial towns of Lanarkshire, Ayrshire and Dumfries. The clays of the River Clyde made bricks. Today, they vie with modern man-made materials – concrete, glass and steel – for attention.

Just 200 years ago, the landscape around the bustling port of Glasgow was little different from the rest of southern Scotland. But in 1801 someone stumbled across an unprepossessing-looking rock in a field near Airdrie that would soon transform the whole area into 'the workshop of the Empire'. Blackband ironstone, the chief ingredient with coal for making iron and steel, saw Glasgow expand sevenfold in under a century – to a staggering one million souls – easily outstripping the ancient capital Edinburgh. And although the ironworks and coalmines have all now closed, and in their wake the car factories and shipyards also, Glasgow and its life-force, the Clyde, continue to thrive, thanks largely to the coming of the 'sunrise' industries, notably electronics; now Strathclyde is known as 'Silicon Glen'.

Drumlanrig Castle, Dumfriesshire

Glasgow was a 'workshop' once; today it is more a 'playhouse', a vibrant modern city with an engaging, multi-ethnic diversity, a city that appeals and appals in equal measure – shiny centre and shadowy suburbs. But beyond the great city, and within easy reach, lie such natural gems as Loch Lomond, the largest single stretch of inland water in Britain, Leadhills, 'God's treasure-house in Scotland', and the islands 'doon the watter', Bute, Arran and the Cumbraes. Man's best endeavours are evident in the many castles and country seats dotted about the land, the ancestral seats of some of Scotland's greatest dynasties – Douglas, Hamilton, Maxwell, and of course Robert Bruce himself, born and bred beside Ayrshire's sandy shore within chipping distance of the ninth green at Turnberry!

George Square & City Chambers, Glasgow

What began in George III's reign (1760-1820) as an elegant square surrounded by fine houses had, by Queen Victoria's death in 1901, become Glasgow's civic square, the hub of the city's political, commercial and social life. The impressive City Chambers – Victoria herself laid the foundation stone in 1883 – preside over the square from the eastern side. Peering down from his lofty central perch, somewhat ironically, is Sir Walter Scott, a native of Edinburgh.

City Centre, Glasgow

Looking down on the city centre, the eye is drawn first to the red rectangle of George Square, Glasgow's civic centre. But it is the three enormous 'seas' of glass shrouding Glasgow's three main railway terminals that hold the attention most. The grandest of them all, St Enoch's Station (top left), was demolished in 1977 and replaced by the huge L-shaped marquee that is the St Enoch Centre, but Central Station (top right) and Queen Street Station (bottom right) remain.

Glasgow University

Gilmorehill, overlooking the River Kelvin, should have become a necropolis for wealthy Glaswegians. Instead, in the 1860s the place became the new home of Glasgow University. George Gilbert Scott's two quadrangles dominate this aerial view; so too the lofty south tower and the massive Bute Hall in its shadow. The court to the left was originally open, giving a view out to Professors' Square; Lord Kelvin (1824-1907), who gave us the first trans-Atlantic communication cable and the Kelvin scale of temperature, lived at No. 11. The prospect was closed in the 1920s when the War Memorial Chapel was built. Beyond lie the tree-fringed circular Reading Room of 1939, and the Corinthian-columned Wellington Church of 1882.

River Kelvin and Kelvingrove Park, Glasgow

Kelvingrove Park was created in the 1870s as a place where Glaswegians could 'take a breather'. Initially they were allowed only to stroll around the tree-clad slopes, but latterly sporting activities have been encouraged, including most recently this skateboard arena.

Park Terrace and Park Circus, Kelvingrove, Glasgow

This green hill overlooking the River Kelvin was to have been Glasgow University's new home when the medieval campus in High Street was purchased by a railway company in the 1860s. The plan came to naught. Instead, Charles Wilson, architect, was invited to design upmarket 'des-reses'. The graceful curves and flamboyant façades of his terraces are Glasgow's answer to Edinburgh's 'New Town'.

Cardonald, Glasgow

The seemingly relentless expansion of Glasgow reached Cardonald, on the Paisley Road West, south of the Clyde, in the 1930s, bolstered chiefly by Rolls-Royce building their huge aero-engine factory at nearby Hillington. Glasgow Corporation's four-in-a-block flatted 'cottages' were joined by four medium-rise tower blocks in the late 1960s.

The River Clyde above Whiteinch

The Clyde slithers snake-like west through Glasgow on its search for the open sea. To either side lie the slipways and cranes, tell-tale signs of the city's greatest industry – ship-building. By 1900, the Clyde was producing a fifth of the world's ships, and the phrase 'Clyde-built' had become synonymous with quality.

Glasgow Science Centre and the River Clyde

On the site of the old Pacific Quay and Prince's Dock, in Govan, stands the Science Centre, Glasgow's latest visitor attraction, built to herald the new millennium. The gleaming titanium-clad 'hothouse of learning' is packed with exhibitions, a 'science mall' and planetarium, whilst the shiny pod beside it houses the IMAX Theatre. If you like heights, then a trip up the 492 ft (150 m) high Glasgow Tower, the only building in the world that turns through 360°, is for you.

Quayside Flats and the River Clyde, Glasgow

The shipyards along the River Clyde, downstream from the City Centre, have mostly gone. Upmarket flats are now rising up to take the place of the cranes and slipways – a sure sign that Scotland has almost shed its 'industrial' skin.

Clyde Auditorium (the Armadillo), Glasgow

In 1997 the Clyde Auditorium was added to the Scottish Exhibition and Conference Centre (SECC), opened in 1985 on the site of the old Queen's Dock, in Finnieston. The building, with its eight overlapping metal plates, was soon christened 'the Armadillo' by Glaswegians. But whereas the American animal burrows into the earth, this 'Armadillo' stays above ground and positively buzzes with life.

Dennistoun Tenements, Glasgow

Glasgow's stone tenements are a testament to the huge expansion of the city in Victorian and Edwardian times. In the 60 years from 1841, the population of the 'workshop of the Empire' mushroomed from 275,000 to around the million mark. Dennistoun, in the East End, was developed to help meet the housing crisis. Its red and pale yellow sandstone four-storeyed blocks, forming neat oblongs, were designed to attract middle-class tenants, but the East End struggled to compete with the city's posher west side, and the well-to-do working class moved there instead.

Robroyston and the Red Road Flats, Barmulloch, Glasgow

Were William Wallace to return today to the place of his capture, he wouldn't recognise it; in 1305, Robroyston (left), on Glasgow's north-east outskirts, was open country dotted about with the odd fermtoun. But after World War I, the need to build 'homes for heroes' brought builders to it 'big time'. First they built neat two-storey villas with gardens, and after World War II four-storey tenements set in communal grounds. Then in the 1960s they built the notorious Red Road Flats (above); the tallest in Europe, each 31-storeyed 'high-rise' (over 40 floors were originally projected) housed a population the size of Dingwall! They are shortly to be demolished, and the residents are coming back down to earth.

Glasgow Green, the River Clyde and City Centre, Glasgow

The River Clyde threads its way through Glasgow, from Glasgow Green (foreground), where the original settlement began over 1000 years ago and westward past the eighteenth-century Merchant City (right). It flows under a series of road, rail and pedestrian bridges which link the north and south of the city centre, and onward to the lower reaches of the great river. For centuries, the Clyde was a broad and shallow river, but since the 1770s, when engineering problems were overcome and the Clyde was deepened and made navigable, it became the city's major artery and allowed Glasgow to expand and flourish.

Glasgow Cathedral

Around AD 600, St Kentigern – or Mungo
as he was more affectionately known –
built his church in a place called Glasgau,
'the green hollow'. In the thirteenth
century, his successors as bishops of
the vast diocese of Strathclyde built
a great cathedral. It stands yet, the
only medieval cathedral on the Scottish
mainland to have survived the
Reformation of 1560 virtually complete.

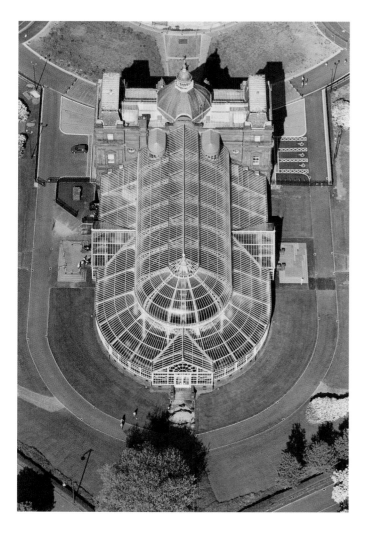

People's Palace, Glasgow Green

The late Victorian People's Palace was built specifically for the
people of Glasgow's East End as a pleasant environment in which
they could 'improve' themselves, physically and intellectually.
They still can – and do – along with the rest of Glasgow, for the red
sandstone building now houses a museum devoted to the city's story.
But if you tire of looking at Billy Connolly's original 'Banana Boots',
there is always the splendid glass-covered Winter Garden behind
the Palace to admire instead.

Townhead, Glasgow

Things started going wrong for Townhead, the upper part of the medieval town, after the Reformation of 1560.
The city's centre of gravity shifted westward to the Merchant City, and into the vacuum moved the factories and slums
that were the hallmark of the industrial revolution. Glasgow's 'green hollow' became a darker shade of grey.
Then came the motor car, and in the 1970s and '80s new roads swept away the detritus,
creating Glasgow's answer to Birmingham's 'Spaghetti Junction'.

Cumbernauld

Cumbernauld New Town was seen as 'the dream on the hill' when construction work began in the late 1950s.
Clydesiders queued in their thousands to relocate there. At its heart stood a huge citadel-like structure comprising
'highways and walkways, layers and ledges promising shelter, warmth and family freedom'. Around this concrete hive
swarmed low-rise housing punctuated by the odd tower-block. The estate names – Kildrum, Muirhead Park,
Ravenswood and the rest – conjured up images of rural idylls far removed from reality.

Pollok House and Pollokshields, Glasgow

The Maxwells came to Pollok in the thirteenth century, but the impressive residence gracing the north bank of the
White Cart Water dates from the eighteenth. By 1900, however, the Maxwells found themselves surrounded by suburban Glasgow,
and in 1966 they gave their family home to the city fathers. Pollok House and Park are now enjoyed by the many, not the few.
Glasgow's middle class discovered Pollokshields, to the north-east of Pollok House, in Victorian times.
They covered the fields with large villas, each set in its own compact grounds.

Prestwick Golf Course, Prestwick & Ayr

The green machair behind Ayrshire's sand-fringed coastline makes ideal golf courses.
Prestwick Golf Course (foreground) is one of the finest. It is also among the most historic,
for the first ever Open Championship was played there in 1860. Golf links continue to hug the
shore beyond the town of Ayr until the steep cliffs of the Heads of Ayr intervene to make
life impossible even for the most intrepid of golfers.

Heads of Ayr Leisure Park

The holiday complex hugging the sloping ground above the Heads of Ayr began as a navy training camp in World War II.
But once the war was over, HMS *Scotia* became Scotland's one and only 'Butlins'. The Redcoats wore kilts, and the campers
were woken not by 'hi-de-hi' blaring out from the tannoy but by pipers touring the chalets.

Isle of Arran and Holy Island

The Isle of Arran, in the Firth of Clyde, is Scotland's landscape in miniature. The north end (in the distance) shares with the Highlands a rugged mountain grandeur, whilst the southern half (in the foreground) has an altogether softer Southern Uplands feel about it. The pleasing sweep of Lamlash Bay, with its fish farm, shelters behind Holy Island, whilst out from Brodick Bay beyond steams the ferry to the mainland.

Brodick Castle, Arran

Brodick's red sandstone walls and grey-slated roofs contrast picturesquely with the green grounds girdling it. Brodick was a stronghold of the Hamiltons, who emerged as leading power-brokers around 1500. The lofty battlemented tower in the foreground dates from that time. Since then the earls and dukes have come and gone; now its master is the National Trust for Scotland.

Mountains of Arran, with Goat Fell in the distance

The National Trust for Scotland is also master of Goat Fell (top centre), at 2867 ft (874 m) the highest peak in the mountain range that dominates north Arran. The name may derive from the Norse *geit-fjall*, 'goat mountain', but another possibility is 'windy mountain', from the Gaelic *gaothaich*, 'windy'. Either is perfectly possible, for goat herds were once common across the Scottish Highlands – and many a walker will testify to the wind's presence today.

Burns Monument, Gardens & Brig o' Doon, Alloway

Alloway without Robert Burns has been likened to the Sahara without sand, and the birthplace of Scotland's national bard has
become something of a shrine to the great wordsmith. The 'auld clay bigging' where he was born on 25 January 1759 is just out of shot,
but the circular Monument erected to his memory in 1823 is visible. In the ornamental garden beside it, the visitor will find a statue
to boozy Tam o' Shanter, undoubtedly Burns' best-remembered character. The dying Burns wrote 'Tam o' Shanter' in a single
day in 1796 in far-off Dumfries, but the image of the hump-backed Auld Brig o' Doon (top right) had clearly remained with him,
for this is where he chose to end the epic tale of Tam and his night-time encounter with the witches in auld Alloway Kirk:

Now do thy speedy utmost, Meg,
And win the key-stane o' the brig:
There at them thou thy tail may toss,
A running stream they darena cross.

Culzean Castle

'Bird neuk' is an apt description of the rocky perch of Culzean (Gaelic *cuil eun*). And perched alongside the birds these
past eight centuries has been a castle of the Kennedy clan. The present edifice isn't really a castle at all, but a handsome country mansion
built for the 10th Earl of Cassilis barely 200 years ago. Two of Scotland's great architects and artists, Robert Adam and Alexander Nasmyth,
combined to create a house and landscape worthy of that remarkable 'Age of Enlightenment'.

The Mull of Galloway

The most southerly tip of the Rinns of Galloway, the Mull of Galloway, is also the southernmost tip of Scotland.
From the lighthouse on this exposed headland one looks out over the treacherous North Channel southward to the Isle of Man
(pictured top right) and westward to Ireland. The name 'Galloway' derives from the Gaelic *gall-gaidhel*,
'land of the stranger Gaels', after the invaders from across the water.

Portpatrick, Galloway

In summer, visitors swarm around Portpatrick, admiring the pretty white-washed houses lining its streets.
They are drawn to the seaside town by the nearby rugged coastline and challenging golf links. But not since 1848 have they been able
to embark there for Ireland, 20 miles (32 km) to the west. No more do herds of imported Irish cattle stampede up those streets,
nor soldiers heading for Ulster march down them. Portpatrick is peaceful now.

Threave Castle, Stewartry

Legend tells that Threave Island, on the River Dee, was the home of the ancient Celtic rulers of Galloway a thousand and
more years ago. Today there is no trace of their fortress. The tall, forbidding tower-house that now dominates the island was built
for Sir Archibald Douglas, soon after he became Lord of Galloway in 1369. Better known to history as Archibald 'the Grim' because
of 'his terrible countenance in warfare' – he dislodged the English from their last bolt-hole in the West March,
Lochmaben Castle – Lord Archibald died peacefully at his island residence on Christmas Eve, 1400.

Kirkcudbright & The River Dee, Galloway

Pretty Kirkcudbright ('Kirk-Cuthbert) has had its 'ups' and 'downs' since 1330. Then it had a royal castle and a friary. Both had gone by the 1590s when Provost MacLellan of Bombie built himself a fine residence at the head of St Cuthbert's Street. Daniel Defoe, visiting in 1724, wrote of 'a harbour without ships, a port without trade, a fishery without nets, a people without business'. The arrival of artists of the calibre of Peploe, Hornel and Jessie King has since given the sleepy town the feel of an artists' paradise.

The River Nith and Solway Firth

The waters where the Nith (bottom left) runs into the Solway may look placid but down the centuries they have taken their toll of the unwary caught out by the swift-running tides. In medieval times those waters came to Scotland's defence time and again; in 1307 Edward I of England died on the southern (English) shore (top right), preparing yet again to invade. Mighty Caerlaverock Castle stands amid the trees on the far side of the River Nith. In the far distance are the four great cooling towers of Chapelcross nuclear power station, among the U.K.'s first, opened in 1960.

Caerlaverock Castle

Caerlaverock – 'fort of the skylark' – has stood beside the Solway Firth these past eight centuries. The ancient stronghold of the Maxwell earls of Nithsdale has a history of lordly residence and wartime siege. In 1300, mighty Edward I of England, 'Hammer of the Scots', appeared in person before its walls. A herald in his retinue described it as being 'in shape like a shield, for it had but three sides round it, and good ditches filled right up to the brim with water' – so strong, in fact, 'it feared no siege'. Nevertheless, Edward captured it in under two days.

The Lowther Hills and Wanlockhead

The Lowther Hills were formed 450 million years ago. Later vulcanic movements formed fissures into
which flowed the mineral ores that have since earned this bleak place its nickname 'God's treasure-house in Scotland'.
Gold drew men to this remote spot time and again – the Crown of Scotland was created from it in 1540 – but it was
lead that filled the wage-packet. The mining villages of Wanlockhead (above) and Leadhills were the centres
of a profitable industry that ended just 50 years ago. Wanlockhead has another claim to fame –
at 1500 ft (450 m) above sea level it is Scotland's highest village.

The River Clyde, Upper Clyde Valley

The River Clyde meanders through Clydesmuir, sometimes pointing north, sometimes west,
sometimes even south back to the Lowther Hills whence it came. From the air, it is easy to see why Scotland's most important
river measures over 125 miles (200 km) long from source to mouth when a crow could fly the same route in under 40 miles (65 km)!
The main west-coast railway line from Glasgow to London makes an appearance on the right.

New Lanark

In 1785, nothing man-made stood beside the River Clyde directly below the dramatic Falls of Clyde. In that year, the entrepreneur David Dale established a textile town there; he called it 'New Lanark', to distinguish it from the medieval town standing on the hills behind. Within 10 years, New Lanark was the largest cotton factory in Britain, employing 2000 people in giant mills and housing them in neat rows of tenements. Dale experimented with new social and educational ideas designed to improve the lot of his workforce. His son-in-law, Robert Owen, took this enlightened industrial philanthropy to new heights, abolishing child labour, building a school for their formal education, and an Institute for the Formation of Character, where they learned to sing and dance. All these buildings still stand remarkably complete – a lasting monument to Scotland's industrial revolution.

Bothwell Castle and The River Clyde

Beside a winding in the River Clyde stands mighty Bothwell Castle, one of the outstanding
monuments of medieval Scotland. During the bloody Wars of Independence with England (1296-1356),
Bothwell endured siege upon siege, passing between the protagonists much like a bone between two dogs.
The original 'stalwart toure' (left) was largely destroyed in 1337 to prevent the castle being garrisoned by the English.
It fell to Archibald 'the Grim', 3rd Earl of Douglas, to rebuild the ancient stronghold of the Morays.

Strathclyde Park

The Clyde valley between the towns of Motherwell (centre left) and Hamilton (far right) was once a pleasure-ground for the haughty Hamilton dynasty. Today, Hamilton 'Low Parks' is the people's park – 1000 acres (400 ha) of woodland and open space, lakes and recreational facilities, including a fine theme park beside the man-made Strathclyde Loch.

Stirling, Argyll & the Isles

Stirling has been described as 'the brooch clasping Lowlands and Highlands together', for the ancient royal burgh beside the meandering River Forth guarded a vital 'gateway' between the two in centuries gone by. Whichever way the traveller approaches Stirling, whether from the Highlands to the north or from the Lowlands to the south, you head towards a very different landscape – one green and pleasant, the other rugged and mountainous.

The River Forth, one of Scotland's great rivers, makes that journey and reflects that transition. It oozes from its source in the shadow of mighty Ben Lomond, way to the west of Stirling, masses and gathers its strength in the lochs of Chon and Ard, then threads eastward across the central valley between the mountained Highlands and the more gently rolling hills to the south until the dense peat mosses of the Stirling basin slow it almost to a trickle. Below Stirling, the river continues its stately progress to the Firth of Forth and the North Sea beyond.

Westward from Ben Lomond lies a different Highland landscape, one lacking that awesome rugged grandeur, but taking its majesty more from the interplay between land and sea. Long, sinuous sea lochs penetrate far inland, whilst a myriad of isles, great and small, inhabit the shimmering seas to the west. An entire book could easily be filled with fascinating aerial views of Argyll and the Isles. They are stunning to look at, beguiling to explore, and wonderful havens of peace in an increasingly hectic world. Little wonder the founding fathers of Christianity – St Columba, St Brendan and the rest – made their homes there 1500 years ago, in idyllic island retreats such as Iona and Tiree. The peninsulas and islands are also a paradise for wildlife; seabirds and seals happily share the rocks and dine on the plentiful marine harvest in the blue-green waters offshore.

Unsurprisingly, given Stirling's pivotal role in the landscape, the region is steeped in history. Four major battles were fought on the flat carseland below mighty Stirling Castle, including William Wallace's resounding victory over Edward I of England at Stirling Bridge in 1297, and Bannockburn in 1314 where King Robert the Bruce sent Edward II home 'to think again'.

Ben Cruachan, Argyll

Both battlefields are revered today as national monuments. Another national monument, the Antonine Wall, reaches across the rolling hills of the Central Belt from Forth to Clyde. The landscape dictated the route of Imperial Rome's most northerly frontier, built by Emperor Antoninus Pius's legions in the second century AD, as it would later guide the eighteenth-century canal builders and the nineteenth-century navvies constructing the main railway link between Glasgow and Edinburgh. Way to the west, in Argyll and the Isles, are monumental reminders of Scotland's ancient prehistoric past, most beguilingly in tranquil Kilmartin Glen, where temples and tombs abound.

But whilst man might have scratched the surface, the land beneath remains unyielding. It is not the monuments of man that impress so much as the monuments of nature – those mountains and moors, lochs and burns. Today Ben Lomond and Ben Ledi, The Cobbler, Stuc a' Chroin and other towering peaks have joined with Loch Earn, Loch Katrine and the other 'great lakes' to form Scotland's first National Park, Loch Lomond and The Trossachs, designated in 2002. Centred on its southern 'gateway' at Balloch on Loch Lomond, the Park reaches westward into Argyll, northward to Crianlarich, in Ben More's shadow, and eastward to the Lake of Menteith, Scotland's only 'lake'; in all, 720 square miles (1865 square kilometres) of sheer natural beauty.

The River Forth, just East of Stirling
The River Forth meanders east from Stirling to the Firth of Forth, past the town of Alloa (top left),
the chimneyed Longannet Power Station and the steamy cooling towers of Grangemouth on its southern shore. In 1297,
the Forth's sluggish waters bore the blood of Englishmen to the open sea, slain by Wallace at Stirling Bridge.

Wallace Monument
The National Wallace Monument (left) thrusts up from Abbey Craig, near Stirling, where in 1297 William Wallace planned his
victory over the English at the battle of Stirling Bridge. The view from the top of John T Rochead's 220 ft (67 m) high rocket-like tower,
up those 246 steps, is dramatic, looking over the place where Lowlands and Highlands meet. The Monument took eight years to build,
and the inauguration ceremony took place on 11 September 1869, the 572nd anniversary of Wallace's famous victory.

Falkirk Wheel

In the 'good old days', barges had to navigate through 11 locks to pass from the Forth & Clyde Canal
to the Union Canal 115 ft (35 m) above, a journey that took the best part of a day. Today, thanks to the Falkirk Wheel,
that trip takes a couple of minutes! The spectacular wheel, opened in 2002 as part of British Waterways' Millennium Link Project,
is an exceptional feat of engineering – the only rotating boat lift in the world. Costing nearly £90 million, the 'wheel' is in fact
a massive gondola which transports whole barges or pleasure craft. Boats are manoeuvred into a kind of cradle which
contains around 300 tonnes of water, which then slowly rotates from one canal to the other.

Forth & Clyde Canal, West of Banknock

Four lines of communication stride across Scotland's Central Belt in this view. The oldest is the Antonine Wall, Imperial Rome's most
northerly frontier, faintly visible climbing Croy Hill (centre left), close beside the Glasgow-Edinburgh railway line. The A803 (centre right)
heads towards Kilsyth, but centre stage is the ribbon-like Forth & Clyde Canal, built in the 1780s and still going strong.

Bannockburn

The saltired flagstaff and cairn were erected first, in 1870, then the rotunda, in 1962, and finally the fine equestrian statue of Robert the Bruce himself, in 1964. All remember Bruce's great victory over Edward II of England, fought close by in June 1314 – 8000 Scots up against twice as many English. The Scots, led by Bruce's younger brother, Edward, and the Earls of Douglas and Moray, emerged from the early morning mist, leading their infantry downhill to the massed ranks of the 'auld enemy' drawn up beside the Bannock Burn. The headstrong Earl of Gloucester cavalry-charged them, only to be unhorsed and crushed beneath the advancing spears. Seizing his chance, Bruce unleashed his own brigade of Highlanders. They rampaged down the slope. The English fled across the burn. Many were drowned, others cut to pieces. Over 1000 Englishmen never saw the end of that Midsummer's Day. For Bruce, it was his reign's defining moment.

Stirling Castle

Mighty Stirling Castle sits atop its rocky perch, commanding the countryside for miles around. So pivotal was the royal fortress's position that it brought the English here time and again during the Wars of Independence, and two great battles, Stirling Bridge (1297) and Bannockburn (1314), have been fought in its shadow. Deep in shadow here is the castle's Upper Square (centre) around which are ranged the most important buildings, including James IV's Great Hall, now restored. Bonnie Prince Charlie was the last to besiege the stronghold, in 1746. Ballengeich Hill, where he mounted his guns, is now a cemetery.

Lake of Menteith & Inchmahome Priory

Tree-clad Inchmahome became the island home of Augustinian canons in 1238, invited to settle in this remote spot 'far from the councourse of men' by the Earl of Menteith. The holy men built a church, and to its south a square cloister, around which they lived and worked. When not at prayer or sleeping, they read, toiled in the grounds or fished on the lake. The canons have long gone, but the fishermen are still here.

Loch Ard, Trossachs

The view west over forest-lined
Loch Ard towards cloud-capped
Ben Lomond – 3195 ft (974 m)
high and the most southerly
Munro in Scotland – is simply
stunning. The bracken-clad
slopes of the Trossachs make
their appearance stage-right,
and behind Ben Lomond's
shoulder range the distant
Argyll peaks – Ben Vorlich,
The Cobbler *et al*. Loch Lomond,
the largest expanse of inland
water in Great Britain, lies out
of sight behind Ben Lomond.
The natural grandeur of the area
was formally recognised in 2002,
as Scotland's first National Park –
Loch Lomond and The Trossachs.

Above Ben More near Crianlarich

Britain's mightiest mountain peaks loom out of the wraiths of mist covering the glens and moors far below.
This dramatic view, looking north-west from above Ben More (3851 ft / 1174 m), on the northern fringe of Argyll,
towards Ben Nevis (right), at 4408 ft (1344 m) the highest mountain in the British Isles, portrays the Scottish Highlands
at their wildest and most inhospitable best – a dark, alien land inhabited by creatures with strange-sounding names,
such as Buachaille Etive Mòr, Sgurr Dhearg and Stob Coir' an Albannaich.

Loch Lomond – the Islands of Inchcailloch and Clairinsh in the foreground

For sheer beauty there is nothing to rival Loch Lomond. For sheer statistics too,
Loch Lomond takes some beating – the largest stretch of inland water in Britain, and at 22½ miles (36 km) long
the third-longest in Scotland, after lochs Awe and Ness. Most of its 30 islands are clustered in the southern third,
and range from good-sized inchs, such as Inchcailloch, 'island of the nuns', to tiny crannogs.

'Loch Lomond Shores'

'Loch Lomond Shores', in Balloch at the south end of Loch Lomond, is the principal 'gateway' into the Loch Lomond and The Trossachs National Park. The impresssive main building, said to have been inspired by an ancient castle but looking more like a prehistoric broch tower, houses six floors of education and leisure facilities, and a great view over the loch.

Maid of the Loch, Balloch, Loch Lomond

On 5 March 1953 the *Maid of the Loch*, the last paddle-steamer made in Britain – by A & J Inglis of Glasgow – slid down Balloch slipway into Loch Lomond. For the next 28 years she gave pleasure to millions, until withdrawn from service in 1981 and left to rot. In 1992 she was rescued from oblivion and, although still static, is afloat yet, and fast being restored to her prime.

Luss, Loch Lomond

The pretty stone cottages of Luss, roofs neatly slated and gardens just as neatly maintained, cluster round the little wooden pier jutting into Loch Lomond. Luss is very picturesque – almost too picturesque for its own good, as it is often swarming with visitors.

Rothesay Castle, Isle of Bute

From the air, the ancient stronghold of the Stewarts looks for all the world like a giant tortoise that has lost its shell. In its heyday in the thirteenth century, the awesome circular stone curtain wall served as a shell itself, behind which the Stewarts fended off the onslaughts of the Norsemen, Viking descendants who had lorded it over the islands of the Clyde since 1098. In those far-off days, the Norsemen could sail their longships up Rothesay Bay almost to the castle wall itself. Today the bustling town hems in the old 'tortoise' from every side.

Mount Stuart, Isle of Bute

In 1877 a great fire swept through Mount Stuart, the residence of the Stuart Marquises of Bute. From the ashes arose a new, far grander mansion, a veritable 'phoenix from the flames'. Sir Robert Rowand Anderson's red sandstone masterpiece is an essay in Victorian Continental Gothic – pointed-arch lancet windows, steep-pitched dormered roofs and, dominating everything, the lofty octagonal chapel lantern and spire, inspired by La Seo Cathedral in Zaragoza. Little of the original eighteenth-century residence survives – just the dwarfed white-harled wings and the grounds around.

Bute and Kyles of Bute

Bute sits within the jaws of Cowal, separated only by the Kyles ('narrows') of Bute.

Across the Firth of Clyde (left) lies the mainland; over to the right the mountains of Arran.

Bute is an island of contrasts – this north end a rugged brown, the south a carpet of green. Both are owned by the
Marquis of Bute, yet the island once swarmed with Glasgow's working classes coming 'doon the watter' for their annual holiday.

Ferries still bring visitors (the Colintraive–Rhubadoch ferry is pictured to the left) but not as many as in the 'old days'.

Gigha – Looking North East

Gigha – the Vikings named it *Gud-øy,* 'God's Island' – has a feeling of paradise about it.
Bathed by the warm waters of the Gulf Stream, the green and pleasant land has a fertility and climate not normally
associated with the Hebrides. The island is never more alive than in May, when the carpets of bluebells in the woods to the
north of Achamore House (in the centre of the island) vie with brightly coloured rhododendrons for attention.

Kintyre, West of Beinn an Tuirc

The Kintyre peninsula is a long tongue of land that laps the waters separating Scotland from Ulster. We see it here looking north,
'back the way' towards mainland Argyll and the Isles. Last century spruce trees were planted on the slopes of Beinn an Tuirc and Deucheran Hill;
today they have largely been replaced by wind turbines. Both are alien to the area, and both seem strangely out of place.

Tarbert, Argyll

King Robert 'the Bruce' built the castle (centre, above harbour) overlooking East Loch Tarbert in the fourteenth century, to guard
the short land-bridge between Loch Fyne and the Sound of Jura (*an tairbeart* is Gaelic for 'narrow isthmus'). The pretty town itself
sprang up in response to the eighteenth-century herring-fishing boom. Where mighty royal warships once anchored,
hundreds of tiny fishing smacks crammed. Today both are gone, and yachts hold sway.

Inveraray Castle

It has been variously described as 'a grand castle' and 'a vast toy fort'. Whatever view one takes, the view from the air of the mid-eighteenth century seat of the Campbells, Dukes of Argyll, certainly impresses. The 3rd Duke's English architect, Roger Morris, designed the castellated Gothic mansion, and the Edinburgh-born landscape designer, William Patterson, the formal gardens.

Loch Awe and Kilchurn Castle

Loch Awe in medieval times was 'Campbell's Kingdom',
and fifteenth-century Kilchurn Castle, at this north end, was built
by Sir Colin Campbell of Glenorchy, nephew of the Earl of Argyll.
Around the same time, his uncle relocated from Innis Chonnell Castle,
half-way down the 24 mile (39 km) long inland loch,
to Inveraray, beside Loch Fyne.

Loch Fyne, Argyll

Loch Fyne's blue-grey sea waters penetrate deep into Scotland's western
seaboard, from their confluence with the Sound of Bute, far to the south,
to their source at the foot of Glen Fyne (right). The neat town of Inveraray
provides a point of light amidst the gathering clouds, and beneath the
loch swim the herring that have given us Loch Fyne's famous kippers.

Jura – from the North

Deer stalk the hills, but little else stirs on this most rugged of Hebridean islands. The mountain screes and mossy bogs are almost as impenetrable as the rock beneath, whilst the jagged coastline is pockmarked with shingle beaches, towering rock arches and awesome caves; gruesome MacLean's Skull Cave lies in Glengarrisdale Bay (foreground). On the left, between Jura and neighbouring Scarba, lurks the treacherous whirlpool known as the Gulf of Corrievreckan; in the distance loom the famous Paps of Jura.

Stone Circle, Kilmartin, Argyll

A treasure-house of prehistoric temples and tombs awaits the visitor to Kilmartin Glen. They include two neolithic stone circles in Temple Wood – the later circle is pictured here. The Stone Age worshippers were followed by Bronze Age people who converted the temple into a burial cairn, with the stone cist at its core.

Crinan Basin, Argyll

At the west end of the Crinan Canal lies Crinan Basin. From the day it opened in 1801, it has been crammed with boats, from ocean-going vessels avoiding the long sail around the Mull of Kintyre, to fishing smacks and yachts. Pride of place today (bottom left in the basin) is a Clyde 'puffer' that starred as the *Vital Spark* in TV's version of Neil Munro's *Tales of Para Handy*.

Kiloran Bay, Colonsay

Colonsay means 'Columba's Island', and neighbouring Oronsay, 'Oran's Island', but humans have lived here for over 7000 years,
long before those holy men. Our hunter-gathering ancestors came here to collect the hazel nuts, and a cave beside Kiloran Bay
served as one of their homes. Elsewhere on this pleasant island lie relics from later eras – Stone Age temples and tombs,
Iron Age forts and medieval chapels. Most lie not far from the rocky coast and those welcoming sandy bays.

Oban, Kerrera and Mull beyond

Oban Bay, protected from the Firth of Lorn by the natural breakwater of the island of Kerrera, seems perfect for a seaport, yet busy Oban town only emerged in the early nineteenth century. It rapidly became the lifeline to the Isles, and from the Isles to Glasgow and the Clyde. The railway further boosted its thriving economy. One resident to benefit, the banker John McCaig, built 'McCaig's Folly', Oban's answer to Rome's Colosseum, which dominates the townscape from land, sea – and air.

Easdale Island, Argyll

The green-on-grey island of Easdale, peppered with pretty white-rendered cottage rows, is a tranquil haven today, but over a century ago it was a hive of industry. The homes where holiday-makers now spend a few precious weeks were once where slate-working families spent their entire lives, and the small harbour, dotted now with the odd fishing smack and yacht, was formerly crammed with ships laden with slate destined for Glasgow's tenement roofs.

Castle Stalker, Appin, Argyll

The razor-sharp corners and serrated roofs of Castle Stalker contrast with the gnarled lumpen rock – Eilean an Stalcaire, 'Island of the Hunter' – on which the castle stands. The Stewarts, Lords of Appin, built the closed-up, inward-looking tower house around the 1540s to guard the sea-lane from Loch Linnhe into little Loch Laich. The ruined tower was restored in the 1960s, but the owners no longer have defence in mind.

Tobermory, Mull

Tobermory is perhaps Scotland's prettiest town. The palette of colours on the buildings adorning Main Street,
facing the harbour, give the place more of a Mediterranean than a Hebridean feel. Tobermory began as a fishing settlement in 1787,
but became far more popular with tourists, inspired to come here by Mendelssohn's *Hebridean Overture*. Reluctant visitors in earlier times
were Spaniards from the *San Juan de Sicilia*, an Armada galleon whose wreck lies deep in the mud of Tobermory Bay.

South-East Mull

Mull comes from the Gaelic *meall*, 'lump', and there are lots of lumps on this island.
The biggest, Ben More (in the distance), reaches 3169 ft (966 m), the only Munro on any Scottish island other than Skye.
'Big Ben' was formed during the same eruption that created the island of Staffa. The lochs of Uisg and Spelve (in the foreground)
were created millions of years earlier, part of the Great Glen Faultline.

87

Iona from the South (left) & The Village, Iona (above)

Iona, off Mull's south-west corner, will forever be associated with St Columba. The sandy bay at this south end of the island (right foreground) is called Port a' Churaich, 'Bay of the Coracle', supposedly where the holy man and his 12 brethren first came ashore around 563. Columba (in Gaelic *colum cille*, 'dove of the church') created a monastery in Iona's green heart that became a leading centre of spiritual and artistic activity, whose impact was felt far beyond Argyll. That monastic idyll was shattered by the Vikings in 795, and the sandy bay on the island's east side (right), takes its name, Port nam Martir, 'Bay of the Martyrs', from the 68 monks butchered there in 806. The pretty village of Baile Mòr, 'Big Town', now fringes that bay and each year a million pilgrims' feet trudge up the winding Street of the Dead to the abbey.

Staffa

The pillars of cooled lava forming Staffa (the Vikings named it *stafi-øy*, 'pillar island') were formed 65 million years ago,
during an epoch of violent vulcanism deep in the earth's core. This extraordinary natural monument has attracted many visitors,
most famously Felix Mendelssohn in 1829, who was so overawed by the sight and swell of the waters rising and falling
at the mouth of Fingal's Cave (bottom right) that he composed *Hebridean Overture* as a result.

Tiree – Looking South West

The shimmering sand of Gott Bay, near Tiree's east end, is known as *traigh mhór,* 'the long beach'.
Into this bay over the centuries have sailed saints and sinners, seeking shelter from the ever-present winds – St Brendan 'the Navigator'
and St Columba of Iona in their flimsy coracles, and in their wake Viking raiders in their longships. Today Gott Bay is peaceful,
its tranquillity disturbed only by the chirrup of the skylark and corncrake rising from the machair – and the wind, of course.

Coll – Looking North East

Two sandy bays, Feall (left) and Crossapol (right) frame Coll's south-western corner. Beyond them stretches a low, almost lunar,
landscape of gnarled rock thinly covered with tufts of heather and grass. In the far distance (right), across the sea, looms Ardnamurchan Point,
the westernmost tip of the island of Great Britain. Coll's 19,000 windswept acres, now almost deserted, were once quite densely populated.
Residents included the MacLeans, who lived at Breachacha Castle, in the next bay along from Crossapol.

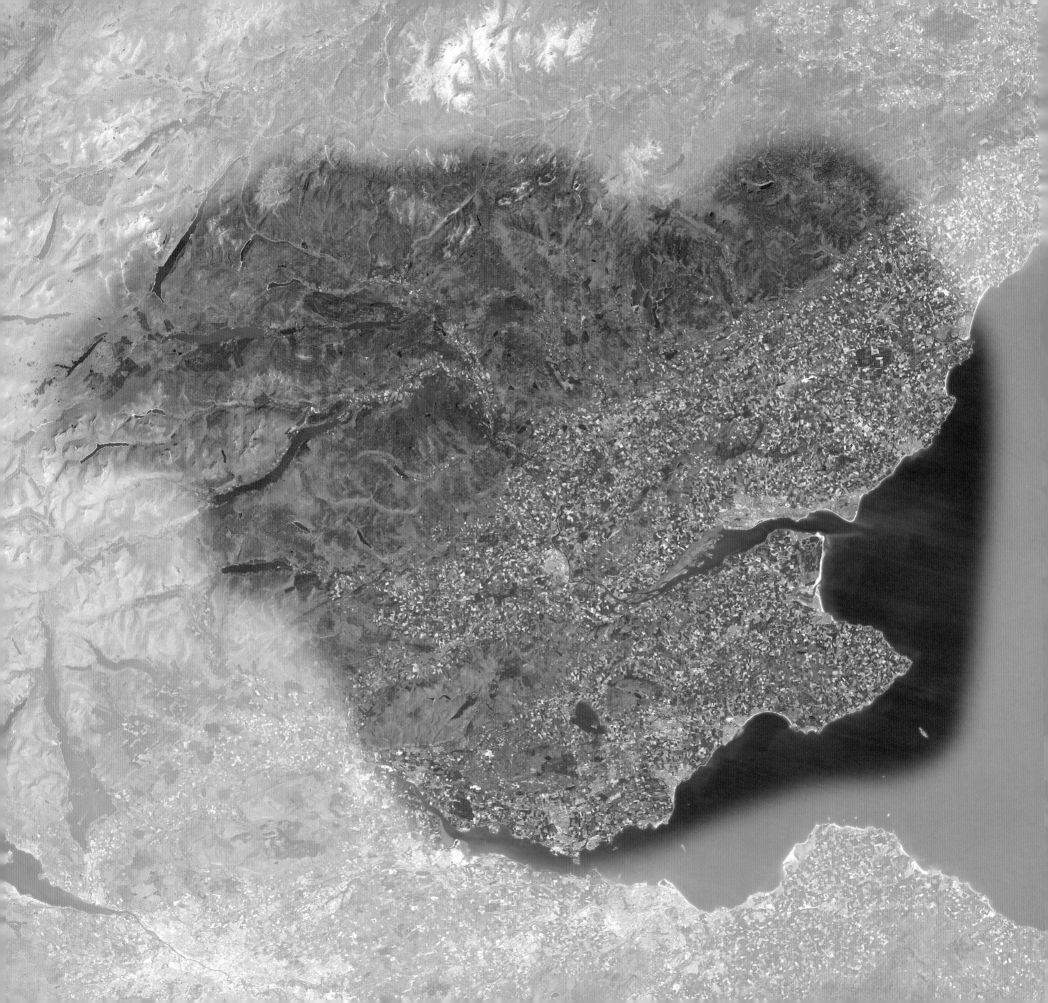

Dundee, Perthshire, Fife & Angus

East-central Scotland has a landscape quite unlike the rest of the country. All across Fife, Angus and the Perthshire plains, from the Firth of Forth in the south to beyond the Montrose Basin to the north, one is conscious mostly of winding rivers threading their way through broad straths fringed with trees and carpeted with fields.

Only in the north, where the Angus glens climb up to meet the dizzy heights of the eastern Grampians, or way to the west, where the lunaresque landscape above Rannoch Moor predominates, do mountains make their presence felt. The Ochils and Sidlaws are no more than gently rounded hills, and the twin peaks of East and West Lomond, in Fife, mere pimples compared with the towering Highland summits. Strathearn and Strath Tay, Howe of the Mearns and the Carse of Gowrie – the names conjure up images of a fertile, fruitful land. Not for nothing is this corner of the kingdom known as Scotland's 'Garden of Eden.'

Strathearn near Crieff, Perthshire

Through this grain-rich landscape flows the Tay, widely acclaimed as Scotland's longest river, 120 miles (193 km) long from its outpouring in the shadow of Ben Lui to its estuary east of Perth. The journey takes 'the silvery Tay' rushing down Strath Fillan and Glen Dochart into Loch Tay, then at a more measured pace round past Aberfeldy and through Dunkeld. Along the way other broad rivers join it, among them the Lyon, the Almond and the Earn. In Strathmore, 'the great valley', several waters compete for pride of place – the Isla, wending westward to the Tay, and the South and North Esk eastward to the North Sea. Here on the coast, high red cliffs and broad sandy bays cut the cornfields short.

Cellardyke, Anstruther Easter, Fife

The region's fertility has bestowed on it a long history of human settlement. Dunkeld means 'fort of the Caledones', associating the place with the confederation of tribes that held out against the might of the Roman Empire. The Caledonians later amalgamated to become the Picts, who acclaimed their new kings on the Moot Hill at Scone. On a Fifeshire headland overlooking the North Sea, the Picts built a church that would in time become St Andrews Cathedral.

The region's prosperity is evident also in the many fine medieval castles and country seats dotted about the landscape, many surrounded by gardens and green parks. The towns likewise tell of long-established wealth, none more so than Perth and Dundee, benefiting from their location on the coast, from where they could trade with mainland Europe. In medieval times these two burghs regularly competed with each other for a place among Scotland's 'big four', alongside Edinburgh, Aberdeen and Berwick-upon-Tweed. 'The fair maid of Perth' still has its medieval charms and grid-like street pattern, whereas Dundee has become more of a concrete hive of commerce and industry. All along the long coastline, from the Firth of Forth to beyond Montrose, is a host of little fishing ports that still bob and clank with fishing boats and pleasure craft. The East Neuk of Fife has some of the most picturesque havens in all Scotland, strung out along the cliffs like a pearl necklace.

The River Earn and River Tay, Perthshire

The meandering River Earn joins the Tay a little downstream of Perth. In the foreground lie the newly harvested
grainfields of Strathearn, and across the Tay stretch the broad acres of the Carse of Gowrie, better known for their fruit.
The little towns of Inchyra and Newburgh are visible to left and right, and the city of Dundee lies in the distant haze.

Loch Tay – Looking South West

Scotland's sixth-largest loch is 15 miles (24 km) from tip to toe, from Killin in the south west to Kenmure in the north east.
Salmon swim in its deep waters, whilst the high ground of Breadalbane, part of the mighty Grampians, hems it in on every side.
The lower slopes of Ben Lawers, 'the echoing mountain', are visible top right; from its summit, on a clear day,
one can see both the Atlantic Ocean and the North Sea.

Blair Castle

Blair Castle has served as the chief residence of the dukes of Atholl for centuries, but there is little that is truly
ancient behind the white-washed veneer. The crow-stepped gables, turrets and embattled parapets – even that imposing
towered entrance gatehouse – are all Victorian, created by David Bryce, the leading architect of his day.

Pitlochry

The pretty town of Pitlochry basks in the autumn sun beside the tree-lined River Tummel. Behind stretch the heather-clad
slopes of the Angus glens – Ardle, Shee, Isla, Prosen, Clova and Esk. Pitlochry has become one of Scotland's most popular holiday centres,
thanks to its proximity not just to the outstanding natural beauty around, but also to man-made Loch Faskally (foreground),
formed as part of a great hydro-electric scheme, and famous for the fish ladder in its dam (centre right).

Perth Centre and The River Tay

The River Tay flows beneath John Smeaton's fine stone bridge (built 1771), then the concrete Queen's Bridge (1960)
and finally the Victorian railway viaduct, on its long journey to the sea. On the far bank stands the prosperous town of Perth,
the spire of St John's, the burgh kirk, rising from the centre of its grid-patterned streets. Beyond lies the green sward
of South Insh (island) where in centuries gone by the burgesses burned witches and honed their archery skills.

Scone Palace

The castellated extravaganza that is Scone Palace, seat of the earls of Mansfield, dates only from 1802,
but the history of Scone reaches far back into ancient times. The family's little mausoleum nestling in the trees behind stands upon
one of Scotland's most important historical sites, the Moot ('meeting') Hill, where the people proclaimed their new sovereign –
among them Macbeth (1040) and Robert the Bruce (1306). Charles II was the last to be crowned there, in 1651.

Dundee – City Centre, Rail Bridge & Tay Estuary

Dundee spreads westward along the north shore of the Tay estuary, its city centre linked to Fife by a road bridge and by the long steel span of the second Rail Bridge (seen here); the remains of the first bridge, which disastrously collapsed in 1879, are visible as stumps in the water beneath. Ring roads ripped the heart out of the old city late last century, leaving the medieval Old Steeple (centre) stranded in a sea of concrete shopping malls.

Dundee – Football Grounds

Cheek-by-jowl in the north-east suburbs of Dundee, two great footballing rivals confront each other across a narrow street – the 'blues' of Dundee FC (founded 1893) at Dens Park and the 'tangerines' of Dundee United FC (founded 1910) at Tannadice. Both clubs drew their supporters from the large workforce brought to the banks of the Dens Burn by the fast-expanding jute industry in the later nineteenth century. The mills have all closed now, but the workers' tenements remain – and the football rivalry continues unabated.

RRS *Discovery* & Discovery Centre, Dundee

The RRS *Discovery* left Dundee in 1901, to earn lasting fame as the vessel that took Captain Scott to Antarctica.
Its unique double hull, inspired by Dundee's famous 'whalers', saved it from being crushed by ice-sheets during that first polar expedition.
After years of neglect, the Royal Research Ship returned home in 1986, where it has helped in the rejuvenation of the city's docks,
after their decades in the doldrums. The adjacent octagonal Discovery Centre, opened in 1993, uses technology as innovative
as that in the *Discovery* itself to tell its *Boy's Own* story of life aboard the famous ship.

Glamis Castle

A broad tree-lined avenue draws you to the pink-grey walls of Glamis Castle, with its spiky battlements and fairytale turrets.
Two very different royal personalities are intimately linked to it – King Macbeth, Thane of Glamis in the eleventh century, and the late
Queen Elizabeth the Queen Mother, born and brought up there in the twentieth. The handsome Jacobean pile was created
for Patrick Lyon, Lord Glamis, to mark his becoming Earl of Kinghorne in 1605.

Montrose Basin and Montrose

A broad tidal lagoon awaits the River South Esk as it meets the North Sea at Montrose.
Its 2530 acres (1024 ha) are a haven for wildfowl and waders, making the Montrose Basin third in importance behind
the great estuaries of the Solway and Forth. The neat town beyond has a long pedigree – the ill-starred King John was
forced to surrender his crown to Edward I of England there in 1296 – but is better known today as a golfing resort.

St Andrews

St Rule's Tower dominates the sprawling complex of St Andrews Cathedral (foreground), headquarters of the Scottish Church in medieval times and the country's major place of pilgrimage. Behind stands the twin-turreted east gable of the once-vast cathedral, and to the left the great cloister court of the cathedral canons. The bishops' castle, where Cardinal Beaton had George Wishart, the Protestant preacher, burned to death in 1546, and where he too was brutally murdered shortly after, hugs the green cliff-top promontory on the right.

St Andrews Golf Courses

There is no finer links golf course anywhere in the world than the Old Course at St Andrews. Founded in 1754,
the Royal and Ancient isn't the world's oldest golf club (the Honourable Society of Edinburgh Golfers was established on
Leith Links a decade earlier); nor was it the first to house the Open Championship (that honour goes to Prestwick in 1860).
Nonetheless, St Andrews is today regarded the world over as the 'home of golf'.

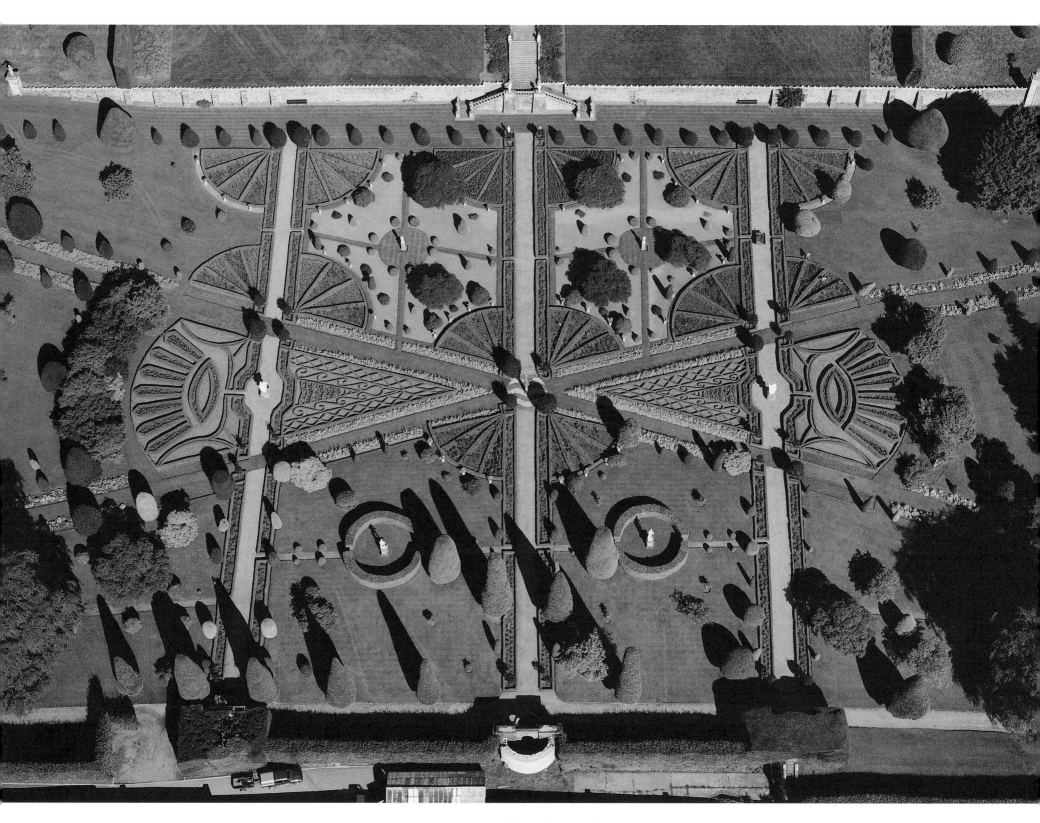

Drummond Castle Gardens

The saltire, Scotland's national flag, provides the design for the formal garden to the south of Drummond Castle, created by John Mylne,
Charles I's architect, in 1630. At its centre stands a fine obelisk sundial, whilst ancient yews and copper beeches give welcome shade.
It is not hard to see why this wonderful sight, created for the 2nd Earl of Perth, is extolled as one of Europe's finest formal gardens.

Tay Road Bridge

The Tay Road Bridge heads south from Dundee across the Tay
estuary to Fife. Before Ove Arup's concrete bridge was opened in 1968,
ferries chugged back and forth across the firth, from Newport-on-Tay
(right) to Dundee; the train ferry linking Tayport (left) to Broughty Ferry,
east of Dundee, closed with the opening of the second Tay Rail Bridge
in 1887. In the distance lies Tentsmuir Forest and the Abertay Sands,
part of the Tentsmuir Point National Nature Reserve.

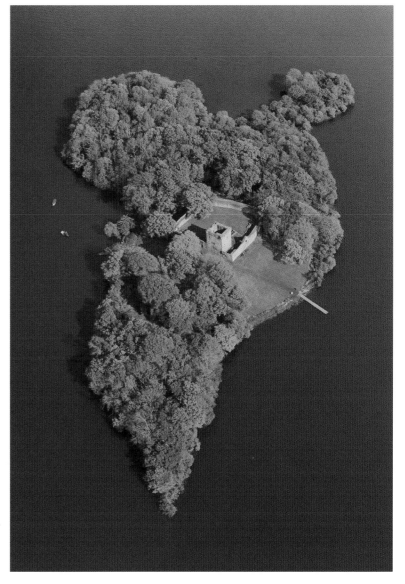

Lochleven Castle

The island stronghold on Loch Leven is associated
with many colourful events, but will be forever linked with
Mary Queen of Scots, held prisoner here in 1567-8, and where
she was persuaded to abdicate in favour of her infant son,
James VI of Scotland and I of England. Mary eventually escaped
her watery prison in May 1568, only to find herself shortly
thereafter a prisoner of her cousin, Elizabeth I of England.

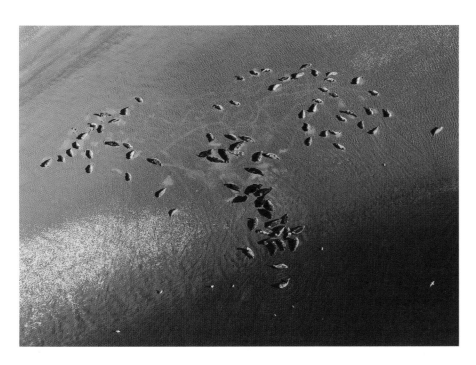

Abertay Sands, Fife

Common seals bask in the shallow waters of the Abertay Sands,
off Tentsmuir Point at the mouth of the Firth of Tay. They are just
one of the many natural attractions waiting to be discovered in the
haven of wildlife and natural beauty that is the Tentsmuir Point
National Nature Reserve.

Pittenweem, Fife

Pretty white-harled buildings with red-pantiled roofs frame the cosy harbour of Pittenweem, still with a healthy complement of fishing boats, though not as many as in the good old days; 17 boats were at their moorings in 1645 when news came through that their crews had been killed at the Battle of Kilsyth. The white three-storeyed fish market on the quayside beside the inner harbour has served the fisherfolk well these past 200 years.

Elie, Fife

Many a medieval pilgrim heading for the shrine of St Andrew in the nearby cathedral city stepped ashore on Elie and Earlsferry's sandy beach, brought there by the ferryman from North Berwick, across the Firth of Forth in East Lothian. The pilgrims have long gone, their place taken by people in pleasure boats.

Crail, Fife

The roots of this royal burgh reach back to the twelfth century when a castle was built on the headland overlooking the harbour. The castle has long gone – it lay at the end of the garden of Crail House (top right) – but the little harbour remains, perhaps the most picturesque of all the pretty villages along the coast of the East Neuk of Fife. The steep, dog-legged Shoregate links the harbour to the High Street behind.

Aberdeen, North-East Scotland & the Central Highlands

Scotland's north-east corner is a land unto itself, a land locked in behind the Grampians' mountained massifs to south and west and the North Sea's watery wastes to north and east. The only natural entrances to this land are the narrow coastal gateways around Inverness and Stonehaven.

The land has a Jekyll and Hyde personality. On the one hand there are the fertile lowland plains, fringed on the north by steep red sandstone cliffs and on the east by great dunes of yellow sand. Here farming and fishing predominate still, despite the vicissitudes of recent times. Tiny harbours nestle into almost every coastal nook and cranny, whilst in the hinterland bustling market towns and neatly planned villages interplay with the patchwork-quilt fields and moorland pastures around. Here corn and cattle are king.

Glen Dee, Cairngorms National Park

On the other hand, there are Grampian's vast mountained wastes, sparsely peopled but abounding with nature and wildlife – the Monadhliath Mountains to the west, the Mounth skirting the southern edge of Royal Deeside, and surpassing all, the Cairngorms, the most extensive and wildest mountain range in Britain, with flora and fauna all its own. This unique sub-Arctic landscape has recently become Britain's latest National Park, and Scotland's second.

Cawdor Castle, near Nairn

In the east, between the mouths of the Dee and Don stands Aberdeen (*aber* means 'river mouth'), Scotland's third-largest city. Its origins reach back far into the Middle Ages, but the seaport flourished as never before during the nineteenth century, thanks in the main to its ship-building industry – to the 'Aberdeen Clipper', a vessel that could outsail the best tea-clippers in the world, and thereafter to those steam-powered fishing trawlers known with affection locally as 'Smokey Joes'. The tea-trade has long departed, and the fishing industry struggles to survive, but now as Europe's 'oil capital', Aberdeen's quayside berths are occupied by the ships serving the off-shore North Sea oil and gas industry.

In years gone by, Aberdeen received the accolade 'silver city of the sea'; now it is more prosaically known as 'the Granite City'. Granite is everywhere, and not just in the buildings of Aberdeen. It is in the mountains and glens, in the walls of mighty medieval castles and more modest post-Reformation tower-houses, in farmhouses and field dykes, in fishermen's cottages and harbour walls. It is even in Balmoral Castle, the Highland retreat of Queen Victoria and Prince Albert that still serves as the royal family's summer holiday home. The advent of the railways in the 1840s first brought the 'royals' back to the Highlands, and it was around then that the present road network emerged. Today, the hitherto land-locked north-east is easily accessed through any number of routes across the once-impenetrable Grampians, bringing the region closer to the rest of the country than at any time in its history. Yet despite this opening-up, the north-east retains much of its identity, its distinctive culture. Grey granite, after all, isn't so easily ground down.

Braemar

In Royal Deeside, just 9 miles from Balmoral, lies pretty Braemar. Each year, on the first Saturday of September, 50,000 people
descend on the oval arena near the village centre for the Braemar Royal Highland Gathering, one of the biggest events of its kind.
There, in front of the royal family, cabers are tossed and bagpipes blown – and everyone has a thoroughly good time.

Lochnagar, Aberdeenshire

Lord Byron's 'steep frowning glories of dark Lochnagar' are depicted here to wonderful effect, as we gaze over the south-eastern fringes of the mighty Grampian Mountains towards fertile Strath Mor and the Lowlands. The distinguished roll-call of those who have climbed the 3789 ft (1155 m) high summit of Cac Carn Beag (right foreground) includes Queen Victoria and Prince Albert, who hiked up from their summer residence at Balmoral Castle, down in the Dee valley to the north (off left).

Balmoral Castle and the River Dee

As soon as they set eyes upon Balmoral, Queen Victoria and Prince Albert were smitten. In 1853, they purchased 'this dear paradise' beside the River Dee, midway between Braemar and Ballater, and invited the Aberdeen architect, William Smith, to design a new residence. The grey granite Scots Baronial castle he built for them here in the heart of Royal Deeside continues to serve as the summer holiday residence of the sovereign.

Crathes Castle and Gardens

Of all the many fine castles and fortified houses in Aberdeenshire, Crathes, near Banchory in Royal Deeside, is among the finest.
Built in the later sixteenth century by Sir Alexander Burnet of Leys, the 9th Laird, the castle is beautiful to behold and beguiling to explore.
His descendants, Sir James and Lady Burnett, the last residents, created the equally enchanting natural setting of secluded
formal gardens and encircling woodland in the twentieth century.

Aberdeen – West of City Centre

'Go west, young man'. And so they did in Aberdeen in the late nineteenth century – west of the city centre (Union Street is just off stage right)
up the Rubislaw Burn to Queen's Cross (the roundabout top left) and to new terraced rows and semi-detached villas,
all built of the grey granite quarried mostly from nearby Rubislaw Quarry (off stage left).

Aberdeen –
The City Centre
and Harbour

Aberdeen lies at the place
where the River Dee (right)
joins the North Sea
(*aber* means 'river mouth').
200,000 citizens live in
'the Granite City', Scotland's
third largest, and the local
grey granite predominates
in this view. So too does
dead-straight Union Street,
the city's main shopping
thoroughfare, constructed
in 1805 and named in honour
of the Union of Great Britain
and Ireland (1801), not
the Union of Scotland and
England (1707). The railway
then arrived in the 1840s,
becoming a vital link to the
wider world for the city and
its busy harbour.

Aberdeen Harbour

The discovery of vast oil and gas reserves under the North Sea in the early 1960s rescued Aberdeen harbour. By then the once-great fishing industry was fast shrinking; so too was ship-building. Into the quayside berths once occupied by 'Smokey Joes' (steam trawlers) and famous 'tea-clippers', such as the *Thermopylae,* slipped the ships supplying off-shore oil-rigs, the pipe-laying barges and survey vessels. Over 40 years on they are still there.

Aberdeen Funfair

The sandy beaches near Aberdeen harbour used to be popular bathing places 50 years ago. Nowadays, despite global warming, Aberdonians find the North Sea breeze just a bit too bracing and prefer the activity of the funfair, amusement arcades and leisure facilities on dry land to a dip in the sea.

Dunnottar Castle

The ancestral seat of the Keiths, grand marischals of Scotland, is spectacular – a lonely plateau thrusting from the precipitous Kincardineshire coast into the chilly North Sea and approachable only over a steep, narrow tongue of land. Of the many remarkable events in Dunnottar's long history, the most memorable came over the winter of 1651-2, when the Honours of Scotland, the nation's Crown Jewels, were hidden there, safe from Oliver Cromwell's clutches.

Stonehaven Harbour

Pleasure craft now lounge around Stonehaven harbour where a century ago
hundreds of fishing boats crammed in like sardines in a tin. Robert Stevenson, Robert Louis Stevenson's grandfather
and famous lighthouse engineer, even had a great rock outcrop obstructing the harbour mouth removed
(the dark 'splodge' beneath the water) to make life easier for the fishermen.

Newtongarry Hill and Huntly, Aberdeenshire

The pretty market town of Huntly (centre left) nestles beside the River Deveron, its waters glistening in the
setting sun on their journey from the Grampian Mountains (off left) to the North Sea. The A96 Aberdeen–Inverness road
threads its way through the patchwork-quilt cornfields up towards the Glens of Foudland, notoriously treacherous in winter.
The peak of Ben Rinnes (2775 ft / 840 m), south-west of Dufftown, looms on the distant horizon.

Inchdrewer Castle, South-West of Banff

A sea of oilseed rape now surrounds ruined Inchdrewer Castle, lairdly residence of a member of the Ogilvie clan. Aberdeenshire is known as Scotland's 'castle country' and the landscape is dotted about with countless examples, great and small. Inchdrewer is typical of those built after the Reformation of 1560 – a good-sized stone tower house overlooking an outer entrance court. Abandoned as a residence by the eighteenth century, Inchdrewer's only resident today is a ghost.

Seatown, Cullen, Moray

The pretty jumble of cottages in Seatown, Cullen, belongs to the heyday of the herring-fishing industry in the nineteenth century. The fisherfolk built their homes gable-end onto the sea so they could 'park' their boats more easily beside them. Cullen Skink, a fish soup made from smoked haddock, has become world-famous.

Pennan, Aberdeenshire

Sandwiched between red sandstone cliffs and blue waters nestles the tiny smuggling-turned-fishing village of Pennan. Its line of white-painted houses are built mostly gable-end onto the sea, each facing the rear of its neighbour, in the traditional fishing village style. A solitary boat shelters in the harbour once crowded with fishing smacks. Look closely and you will see the red public telephone box made famous in the film *Local Hero*.

Sands of Forvie National Nature Reserve & the Ythan Estuary

Broad swathes of sand dune characterise much of Aberdeenshire's east coast from Fraserburgh south to Aberdeen. Undoubtedly the finest are the Sands of Forvie, at the mouth of the River Ythan, Britain's fifth-largest sand-dune system and the least disturbed of all, seen here looking south over Newburgh Bar. The 4 square miles (1018 ha) of dune are constantly changing shape, and man finally abandoned his 6000-year battle to inhabit the area in 1413 after a nine-day-long sandstorm overwhelmed Forvie village. But the Sands are still home to a fascinating natural world, including a large variety of bird species.

Fort George

Three hundred years ago a solitary fishermen's hut was all that stood on the shingle spit jutting into the Moray Firth north-east of Inverness.
Today, one of the outstanding artillery fortifications in Europe stands there – mighty Fort George, named in George II's honour and built as
an impregnable base for his army following the Jacobite defeat at nearby Culloden in April 1746. Fort George took 21 years to complete
and cost over twice the estimate, yet it has never fired a single shot in anger. The guns have gone, but the soldiers remain.

Lairig Ghru, Cairngorms

Towards the end of the last Ice Age many thousands of years ago, mighty sheets of ice gouged out deep defiles in the
granite massif of the Cairngorm Mountains, east of Strathspey. By far the most impressive is Lairig Ghru ('Pass of Drurie'), a narrow,
steep-sided and snow-filled gully 1000 ft (300 m) deep, between the summits of Ben Macdui (left) and Braeriach (right).

Cairngorm Mountains

Cairn Gorm (seen here from the north west), at 4084 ft (1245 m), is not the highest peak in the Cairngorm Mountains –
that accolade goes to Ben Macdui (4295 ft / 1309 m), out of sight beyond the horizon – but it has bestowed its name on the most extensive
area of granite mountain massif in Scotland. Recently designated Scotland's second National Park, the Cairngorms' sub-Arctic summit plateau
is a wintry paradise of alpine plants and rare birds and beasts, including 25 per cent of the endangered species in Britain. The Coire Cas ski
development (pictured here), was first opened in 1961, with construction of a funicular railway following exactly 40 years later.

Ruthven Barracks

Four government army barracks were built across the Highlands after the 1715 Jacobite Rising. They included Ruthven-in-Badenoch, beside Kingussie, designed to house 120 men in two barrack piles, with their officers quartered in the projecting towers. The stable-block was added by General Wade in 1734. At the outset of the '45 Rising, the 12 Redcoats stationed there held out against 300 Jacobites, losing just one man who 'foolishly stuck his head above the parapet'.

Loch Insh and the River Spey, Strathspey

The mighty Spey, the north-east's longest river, travels 107 miles (172 km) from its source high in the
Monadhliath Mountains, south-east of Fort Augustus, to Spey Bay and the North Sea. We see it here writhing snake-like
down Strathspey into Loch Insh, midway between Kingussie and Aviemore. The Insh Marshes RSPB Reserve (centre left)
is one of the most important wetlands in Europe. It provides nesting sites for many bird species in spring,
and roosting and feeding for flocks of geese and whooper swans in winter.

Ben Alder

The setting winter sun glints off Ben Alder's sharp ridge (3765 ft / 1148 m) and sparkles on the still waters of Loch Laidon (left), Blackwater Reservoir (centre) and Loch Ossian (right). In the distance the haunting peaks of Glen Coe are visible. Into this wilderness in the late summer of 1746 crept Prince Charles Edward Stewart, on the run from 'Butcher' Cumberland's Redcoats since his defeat at Culloden many miles to the north. The cave he is reputed to have sought shelter in – Cluny's Cage, named after the clan chief Cluny MacPherson – lies to the left of Ben Alder, near Loch Ericht.

Coire Ardair, Creag Meagaidh

The dark pool of Lochan a' Choire in Coire Ardair (foreground) channels water from the snow-capped slopes around Creag Meagaidh down through Coill a' Choire to Loch Laggan in the shadows beyond. The area is a National Nature Reserve, but Loch Laggan was created by man in 1934 to provide hydro-electric power for Fort William's aluminium smelter way to the west.

The West Highlands & Islands

About 400 million years ago a mighty collision deep in the earth's crust created a great cleft that almost split Scotland in two. Gleann Mòr, 'the great glen', runs for 60 miles (97 km) from north-east to south-west, from the Moray Firth to Loch Linnhe. Many thousands of years ago, giant glaciers scoured and smoothed Gleann Mòr, leaving in their wake three great sheets of water, Loch Lochy, Loch Oich and Loch Ness, the biggest and deepest of them all.

The view down on this corner of Scotland reveals a rugged and remote landscape, evoking images of mighty vulcanic acts and awesome natural forces – Glencoe, the Cuillin on Skye, the Five Sisters of Kintail, Torridon in Wester Ross, and Ben Nevis, at 4408 ft (1344 m) Britain's highest mountain.

Nature's power is evident also in those great lochs which penetrate deep into Scotland's western seaboard, Loch Sunart, Loch Carron, the Sound of Sleat and the rest. It is there too among the islands of the Outer Hebrides, in those sweeps of white strand fringing the green-blue bays of Harris, the Uists and Barra, and on those high cliffs off Lewis's west coast that are constantly pounded by the deep Atlantic swell. There in the Western Isles one looks down also on gnarled grey rocks that are the oldest in the British Isles.

Loch Nevis, Lochaber

Nature overwhelms the region. Human settlement is sparse. It was not always thus. The beguiling Stone Age circles of Calanais signpost a cultured society in the Western Isles five thousand years ago, and the many fortified duns and broch towers tell of wealth worth defending in the centuries before Christ. In medieval times, the descendants of those broch builders constructed forbidding castles for much the same reason. In centuries

Waternish, Isle of Skye

gone by, before the infamous Highland Clearances of the early nineteenth century, the straths and glens teemed with thousands of people, trying their best to tame nature. Then came the landlords with their sheep and their stags, and the crofters were inveigled off the land, forced either to find work in the factories and shipyards on the Clyde or to emigrate to distant lands like Canada and Australia. But here and there the remains of their crofts and townships can still faintly be made out.

Since then, man has reached a compromise with nature. Roads have been laid around lochs, and over high mountain passes. Railways too have appeared, and a great inland waterway, the Caledonian Canal, linking the lochs in the Great Glen with each other and with the oceans beyond. Ferries ply between the mainland and the isles, and bridges have made life easier for the traveller. Today most people live in a few good-sized towns, among them Fort William, beside Loch Linnhe, Portree (*port righ*, 'the king's harbour') on Skye, and Stornoway, capital of the Western Isles, or in little fishing villages, whose harbours cling like barnacles to the rocks. Fishing as a way of life has largely gone, but the villages have metamorphosed into vibrant holiday centres, catering for those searching for peace and natural beauty among the high mountain peaks and remote inland lochs. None leaves disappointed.

Kintail – the Five Sisters

What an awesome sight, gazing westward over the snow-white Five Sisters of Kintail (centre) and down Lochs Duich and Alsh
to the distant Isle of Skye and those other majestic peaks, the Cuillin Hills. The Five Sisters – Sgùrr na Ciste Duibhe (foreground),
Sgùrr na Càrnach, Sgùrr Fhuaran, Sgùrr nan Saighead and Sgùrr na Mòraich (*sgùrr* simply means 'peak') – are well over 2500 ft (762 m) tall,
and are made of tough stuff – Moinian schist. They are also exceedingly old – well over 500 million years old in fact.

Glen Affric
and Loch Affric

Glen Affric is one of the most beautiful Highland glens. Hidden away in the mountains, midway between Gleann Mòr ('the Great Glen') and the western seaboard, over the snow-capped peaks way to the west, the deeply forested glen with its loch offers utter tranquillity for today's more adventurous visitor – outside the deer-stalking season that is. Changed days indeed from medieval times, when kilted Islesmen poured through the glen in search of plunder. In the eighteenth century they drove their cattle down the glen towards the tryst at Muir of Ord.

Loch Ness from the North

Even though Loch Ness rarely exceeds one mile in width, it is second only to Loch Lomond in surface area
thanks to its 23 mile (37 km) length. The first sightings of the loch's most famous resident, 'Nessie', were made in 1932,
coinciding with the building of the A82 trunk road, seen threading along the loch side (right).

Urquhart Castle

Spread over a rocky promontory jutting into the chilly depths of Loch Ness is mighty Urquhart Castle.
For over 500 years great lords held sway from within its walls – Durwards, Comyns, the royal house of Bruce, the MacDonald
lords of the Isles, the Gordons and Grants. When the last garrison marched out in 1690, they blew up the towered entrance gatehouse.
The walls of the Grant Tower (top) came crashing down during a violent storm in 1715.

Glencoe – Bidean nam Bian in foreground

An t-Sròn's serrated edge (foreground) acts as a buttress on the western edge of Glencoe's mountain massive.
Beyond loom Glencoe's giants, with names to match their grim, forbidding appearance – Bidean nam Bian (peaks of the ben),
Stob Dubh (black post) and the twins, Buachaille Etive Mòr and Beag (the great and small herdsmen of Etive). The Three Sisters frown
down upon the Pass of Glencoe and its little Loch Achtriochtan into which the River Coe creeps. Neil Munro, the Scots novelist,
wrote of Glencoe as 'forgotten of heaven and unfriendly to man' – a fitting description.

Ben Nevis – Looking South West

Mighty Ben Nevis towers over Lochaber. Behind its left shoulder lies Loch Linnhe.
Thousands trek to the top of Big Ben's 4408 ft (1344 m) every year, most of them opting for the gentler ascent from
Achintee on the far side. The more adventurous prefer the challenging steeper climb up Allt a' Mhuilinn to this south-western side.
The meteorological observatory visible on the summit was manned day and night for 20 years in Victorian times!

Glenfinnan & Loch Shiel
The River Finnan (foreground) rushes down Glen Finnan, under the viaduct, to Loch Shiel.
Lochaber's high mountains crowd in on every side. History was made here on 19 August 1745 when Prince Charles Edward Stewart arrived
at the head of the loch to begin the fifth, and final, Jacobite Rising. The tall tower beside the loch, erected in 1815, marks the spot where
he raised his father's standard. History was also made here in 1901 when the West Highland Railway built the splendid curved viaduct,
for the 1247 ft (380 m) long 21-arched structure remains Scotland's longest concrete railway bridge.

Neptune's Staircase, Banavie, Fort William

The railway swing bridge carrying the West Highland line from Fort William (off right) to Mallaig is open; so too the road bridge taking the A830. Time now for the boats newly arrived at Corpach, on Loch Linnhe, to begin their ascent of the eight giant locks at Banavie, affectionately known as 'Neptune's Staircase'. Beyond lies the Caledonian Canal which will transport them through the Great Glen, via the three inland lochs of Lochy, Oich and Ness, to Inverness and the Beauly Firth 60 miles (97 km) away. Thomas Telford's greatest engineering feat, opened in 1822, is still going strong.

South Morar, Lochaber – Looking East

Caledonia's tough old hide – Moinian schist – stretches as far as the eye can see in this view over
Loch Beoraid and South Morar. The gnarled rocks accumulated as sediments on a vast ocean floor until,
around 500 million years ago, Europe and America crunched together,
crystallising them and thrusting them high into the air.

Rum – Looking North West

Diamond-shaped Rum has real semi-precious stones embedded in those mountain peaks pictured in the foreground – Askival (centre right)
is the highest at 2663 ft (812 m). Red deer and wild goats roam the high slopes, where golden and white-tailed sea eagles have their eyries.
Down in the valleys beyond, wild ponies pasture, and thousands of Manx shearwater nest in burrows along the rocky coast.
They and the rare alpine plants combine to make Rum an outstanding National Nature Reserve.

Dunvegan Castle, Skye

Near the head of Loch Dunvegan stands Dunvegan Castle, clan seat of the MacLeod chiefs since the thirteenth century and still lived in by them. It has the distinction of being Scotland's longest continuously occupied residence. Much of the present structure, though, is not ancient, the array of battlements and turrets dating back no more than 200 years and designed entirely for show. Even Macleod's great galley has gone from the little bay in which the castle is now reflected.

Boreraig Clearance Village, by Loch Eishort, Skye

Ruined crofthouses sit on the bracken-clad slopes like huge dominoes. Beside them lie derelict barns and empty stackyards within stone boundary walls. Two small cairns indicate where the fields once were, along with the long straight wall that once separated the township from the cattle grazing on the moorland beyond. Boreraig township has a feel of great antiquity about it, and yet it was only in 1853 that the crofters were summarily forced out of their homes by the landlord. Most emigrated to Canada. Onto their abandoned crofts came the sheep.

Cuillin Hills – Looking North

The white-tipped Cuillin Hills almost divide the Island of Skye in two. Only the brown valley of Glen Sligachan interrupts the barrier of volcanic rock. Thirteen gabbro-filled peaks of the Black Cuillin fan out in a curve from Gars-bheinn (foreground) to Sgurr nan Gillean, beside Glen Sligachan, tempting the hardened mountain climber. For the less adventurous are the seven summits of the Red Cuillin, represented here by Glamaig (far right). Beyond this mountain barrier lies the northern half of Skye and far in the distance the Western Isles.

Red Cuillin, Skye

The rounded granite Red Cuillin of Glas Bheinn Mhor (foreground), Beinn na Crò and Beinn na Caillich loom over the Inner Sound, which separates this part of Skye from the mainland beyond. Hugging the shore beyond them is Broadford, and beyond that the new Skye Bridge crossing Kyle Akin. The little island off Broadford Bay is Pabay, derived from papa, the old Irish word for 'father', where one of the founding fathers of Christianity doubtless had his hermitage.

Skye Bridge

The narrow strait between the mainland (left) and the Isle of Skye is known as Kyle Akin, 'Hakon's Narrows', recalling the time in 1263 when King Hakon IV of Norway's vast armada anchored here on its way south to the Battle of Largs in the Firth of Clyde. Centuries ago Skye crofters swam their black cattle across the narrows, and in more recent times ferry boats plied back and forth between Kyle of Lochalsh (left) and Kyleakin. Today the Skye Bridge, opened in 1995, bears the burden, carrying 625,000 vehicles a year 'over the sea to Skye'.

Eilean Donan Castle

Eilean Donan Castle is Scotland's most photographed castle, and yet most of what we see is barely a century old.
'Saint Donan's Isle' had a far from saintly past though, and in 1331, the Earl of Moray and guardian of Scotland had the walls of Mackenzie of Kintail's stronghold 'decorated' with the heads of 50 Highlanders as a warning to others. But during the 1719 Jacobite Rising, government troops blew the place to smithereens, and what visitors so admire today belongs mainly to MacCrae-Gillstrap's grand restoration of 1912-32, including that fine three-arched bridge.

Beinn Eighe, Wester Ross

The Torridon mountains in Wester Ross are the oldest in the British Isles. At their heart towers the mountain massif of Beinn Eighe,
its sedimentary rock sculpted by nature into massive stepped cliffs and pinnacled crags. The sheer unadulterated beauty of Beinn Eighe
was officially recognised in 1951 when it became Britain's first National Nature Reserve.

Loch Maree, Wester Ross

Loch Maree is the 'queen of Highland lochs', a massive sheet of water 12 miles (19 km) long
and surrounded by some of the most majestic mountain scenery in the British Isles. We see it here looking
south-east over its cluster of pine-clad islands to cloud-capped Slioch (3214 ft / 980 m) (centre left) and the mountain
massif of Beinn Eighe (right). The main road link between the Lowlands and the Outer Hebrides once ran along
the north (left) shore to the ferry terminal at Poolewe, until the port of Ullapool was developed in the 1780s.

North Uist

Around 1000 million years ago, Britain's oldest rocks, Lewisian gneiss, finally broke through the earth's crust to form a bleak, desolate landscape, devoid of colour save for the muddy slime. The landscape pictured here in North Uist, looking west over Loch Tarruinn an Eithir, seems not far removed from that primordial scene. Only modern interventions – the A867 trunk road (top right), the odd patch of wood, and the tiny splodges of white that are houses – give the game away.

Calanais Standing Stones, Isle of Lewis

On the west side of Lewis, at the heart of a large complex of megalithic monuments, stand the Calanais Stones, a near-circular ring of 13 boulders of Lewisian gneiss with a monolith at its centre almost 16 ft (5 m) high. A stone-lined avenue defines the approach from the north and single lines of stones radiate from the other three sides. Quite why our Stone Age ancestors built this great monument almost 5000 years ago is a mystery, like so much of their story.

The West Coast of Harris

The Atlantic coastline of the Western Isles is famous for its wonderful cream-white beaches and turquoise seas.
Here in South Harris, beside the Sound of Taransay, we see that landscape to perfection. From the top of Chaipaval,
on the Toe Head peninsula (right) one can see, on a clear day, the Cuillin on Skye and St Kilda way to the west.

St Kilda

Far out in the Atlantic lies the remote archipelago of St Kilda, islands of awesome grandeur – Boreray (left foreground),
guarded by two giant pinnacles, Stac an Armin (664 ft / 196 m) and Stac Lee (564 ft / 172 m), and, looming in the mist beyond, Dun,
Hirta and Soay. The enduring image is of stupefying cliffs rising sheer from the swell to dizzy heights of over 1200 ft (365 m), the highest in the
British Isles, and of countless thousands of seabirds screeching and swirling around their rocky eyries. Humans too have lived here on the island
of Hirta for over 4000 years. There the sinuous village street is lined on one side by houses, with field dykes beyond and those turf-topped
oblong storage 'cleits', peculiar to St Kilda. The large oval enclosure was their graveyard. The inhabitants finally gave up their long
struggle to inhabit the archipelago in 1930 when the remaining 36 islanders embarked for a new life on the mainland.

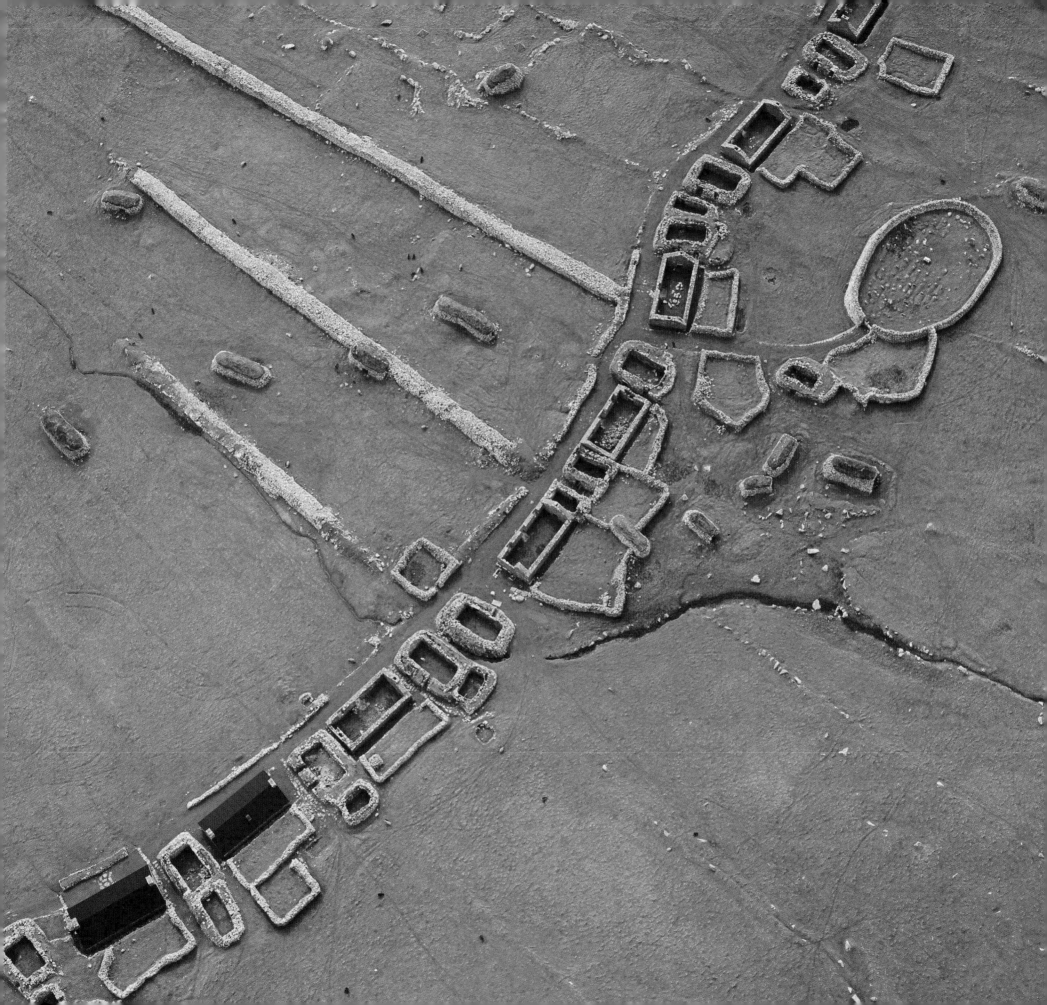

Inverness, Northern Scotland & the Northern Isles

As we soar above northern Scotland and the Northern Isles, the enduring image is of wide-open spaces. They are there in the mountained wilderness of the North-West Highlands, and in that broad carpet of bog covering much of Caithness and eastern Sutherland that we know as the 'Flow Country'. They are there also in the myriad low-lying islands of Orkney and Shetland.

The peaks of Torridonian sandstone that comprise the North-West Highlands are on a grand scale. Suilven, for example, rises almost sheer from its foundations of Lewisian gneiss to a height of 2398 ft (731 m). Grandeur is there also in long sea lochs such as Loch Broom and Loch Eriboll which penetrate far beyond the rock-hard coasts on the west and north. It is there too in the broad firths that slice through the softer sandstones of the east coast – Dornoch, Cromarty and the mighty Moray Firth east of Inverness. Inland, in the straths and glens, lie great sheets of fresh water, none grander than Loch Shin, some 17 miles (27 km) long. Cape Wrath is the most north-westerly point of the British mainland, Duncansby Head the most north-easterly, and Dunnet Head the most northerly. All three defer to a tiny speck of rock at the northern tip of Shetland, for Out Stack alone can claim to be the most northerly point in the entire British Isles.

In this vast natural expanse, human settlement is noticeably sparse. Around 190,000 people live here, the same number as dwell in Aberdeen. Of these, a quarter live in and around the city of Inverness. In Orkney and Shetland, a third of the 43,000 population squeeze into the respective capitals of Kirkwall and Lerwick.

Orkney has the oldest standing Stone Age house in northern Europe, on Papa Westray, and also its best-preserved Stone Age village – Skara Brae, beside the Bay of Skaill. A little inland stand the great stone circles of Brodgar and Stenness, and the monumental tomb of Maes Howe, all built before Stonehenge. In the ensuing Bronze and Iron Ages, as the climate declined, people fought over the fast-shrinking good land. They built fortified structures, including great stone broch towers, uniquely Scottish. Mousa Broch in Shetland is the most complete of all.

Perhaps the folk on the island of Mousa saw the Roman fleet that reached the Northern Isles in AD 43. The men of Mousa certainly saw the marauding Vikings appear, around 800. The Norsemen established a great province reaching south across the Pentland Firth down as far as Dingwall, barely 11 miles (18 km) from Inverness; *thing vollr* is Norse for 'field of the court of justice'. They built farms, like Jarlshof on Shetland, and fine buildings, none more beautiful than St Magnus Cathedral, in Kirkwall. That Viking legacy endures to this day, in placenames and dialects and customs. None of these is apparent from the air, but as we soar over the region, we might reflect on the families who sailed here from Scandinavia all those centuries ago, and who liked it so much they made it their home.

Moray Firth

Two shingle spits jut into the Moray Firth a few miles north-east of Inverness. Chanonry Point (foreground) has a golf course on it, and Ardersier Point (beyond) has mighty Fort George. Ferry passengers crossing from Fortrose and Rosemarkie (far left) originally had to pass through the fort, until the army provided an alternative route south.

Cromarty Firth

A line of oil rigs reaches down Cromarty Firth looking like ships sailing for the open sea. The Royal Navy were the first to exploit the firth's depths, establishing a dockyard at Invergordon (centre left) in 1913. Shortly after it closed in 1956, oil was discovered way out in the North Sea, and many a drilling rig has come and gone from the firth since.

Inverness – Looking North

The city of Inverness (population 42,000) nestles on low ground either side of the River Ness as it flows north into the sea (*inbhir* is Gaelic for 'river mouth'). East of the mouth (right) stretches the Moray Firth, crossed by the splendid Kessock Bridge, opened in 1983 and carrying the A9 north to the Black Isle. The expanse of blue water to the west of the Ness is Muirtown Basin, near where the Caledonian Canal enters the Beauly Firth.

Dornoch Firth and Bridge

The sun sets on the Dornoch Firth, silhouetting the towering peaks of the distant North West Highlands, among them the highest, Ben More Assynt (3273 ft / 998 m). The Meikle Ferry once plied across the firth, just upstream from the present bridge which opened in 1991.

Suilven, Sutherland

Suilven (2398 ft / 731 m) and its neighbouring peaks to the north of Loch Broom –
Cul Mòr (2786 ft / 849 m) stands to the right – may not be the highest mountains in Scotland,
but they are certainly the most amazing. Here most of the Torridonian sandstone has been
swept away by powerful glaciers, leaving behind isolated outcrops, such as the giant limpet
that is Suilven, clinging to its base of gnarled grey Lewisian gneiss.

Loch an Daimh, Wester Ross

The deep-blue waters of Loch
an Daimh, 'loch of the ox',
seen here looking north-east,
still themselves in readiness for
the long journey ahead, down
Abhainn Poiblidh to the
Rappach Water, on through
Glen Einig and leafy Strath Oykel
to the River Shin, there to
be stilled once more by the
hydro-electric dam at Invershin.
Innumerable lochs like Loch an
Daimh combine to create the
most northerly hydro-electric
scheme in Britain.

Geodha na Seamraig, near Cape Wrath

The sandy beach fringing Geodha
na Seamraig ('shamrock cove')
looks idyllic, but remember
we are within 3 miles (5 km) of
Cape Wrath, the often turbulent
north-western tip of the British
mainland. The dull green pasture
of the little croft of Kearvaig
contrasts with the brown
moorland above. The ruined
building was built early in the
nineteenth century by a crofting
family 'cleared' from their home
in an inland glen.

Handa Island, Sutherland

Handa's square mile of moorland serves as a summer holiday camp for seabirds. Most make for the 400 ft (120 m) high cliffs here on the
north-west side, where they can enjoy the breezes coming off the Minch; a few, such as the arctic and great skua, pitch camp on the brown
heath inland. All told, 180,000 birds fly in each summer, including 120,000 guillemots, the largest colony in Britain.
Here they breed before heading off once more to spend winter at sea.

Duncansby Head, Caithness

Duncansby Head is the most north-easterly tip of the British mainland, and the view from the lighthouse,
built in 1924 by David Stevenson, a relative of R. L. Stevenson, is spectacular. In the foreground are the Stacks of Duncansby, and northward
across the treacherous Pentland Firth looms Orkney, with low-lying South Ronaldsay (right) and the hills of Hoy (top left).

Wind Farm, Caithness

The turbines at the Mybster windfarm, south of Tormsdale, dominate the flat peat bogs that carpet much of Caithness. The ecologically rich and diverse 'blanket bog', 20 ft (6 m) deep in places and covering 1544 square miles (400,000 ha), has been dubbed the 'Flow Country', but the watery peat has little economic value. Hence the windfarm, capable of producing sufficient energy to power 27,000 homes – that's more than enough for Caithness.

Dunbeath Castle, Caithness

Dunbeath Castle crowns a narrow promontory jutting into the North Sea. The setting is classic, for many a Caithness headland has a fortress rising from it. Little of the medieval stronghold, though, has survived the various remodellings by later generations. The late afternoon sun picks out the white-harled entrance front, built around 1624 for John Sinclair of Geanies, but with a new front door (1907). Most of the battlemented parapets behind are Victorian evocations of an ancient martial past.

Keiss Harbour, Caithness

No boats lie in the harbour, but four stand on the slipway and fishing tackle is dotted elsewhere about the little fishing village of Keiss. The two-basin harbour was built around 1830 by the British Fisheries Company to take advantage of the herring boom. In its heyday the harbour would have been crammed with herring smacks and the three-storey fishing store beside it piled high with barrels.

Old Man of Hoy, Orkney

The island of Hoy is hilly compared to the rest of low-lying Orkney, and its name derives from the Viking *haey*,
'high island'. The red sandstone cliffs here on its western side rise sheer from the sea to a height of 500 ft (150 m).
Climbing them hasn't proved easy, and the first recorded ascent of the Old Man of Hoy, the rocky pinnacle in the
left foreground, was by Chris Bonington and friends during a live television broadcast in 1966.

Ring of Brodgar, Orkney

The great Ring of Brodgar, on Mainland Orkney, still contrives to impress and overawe the modern visitor,
as it must have been intended to do when built 5000 years ago. It has been estimated that the encircling ditch
took around 80,000 man-hours to dig, let alone the hours of work to hew and erect the 60 tall stones that
originally formed the ring – an enormous communal effort.

The Churchill Barriers, & the Italian Chapel, Orkney

During World War I, the eastern approaches into the naval base of Scapa Flow were blocked by redundant merchant ships, but these proved useless against German U-boats in World War II which sneaked into the Flow on 14 October 1939 and sank HMS *Royal Oak*. Prime Minister Churchill ordered that the three entrances, Holm and Weddell Sound (pictured), and Water Sound (off to the south) be sealed by solid concrete barriers. Those Churchill Barriers continue to provide easy communication between South Ronaldsay, Burray, Glims Holm, Lamb Holm and Mainland Orkney. Much of the construction work was carried out by Italian POWs, who have left another great Orkney legacy behind, the Italian Chapel on Lamb Holm, created from two Nissen huts.

St Magnus Cathedral, Kirkwall, Orkney

St Magnus, Kirkwall, rivals St Kentigern's in Glasgow as the most complete cathedral surviving in Scotland. Yet Orkney was not Scottish when it was built in the twelfth century but Norwegian. The graceful red sandstone building, by far the grandest structure in the Northern Isles and begun by masons travelling north from Durham, is a joy – inside and out. So too is the music regularly performed therein.

Skara Brae, Orkney

The Stone Age village of Skara Brae is truly special – a maze of snug stone houses and covered passageways built over 5000 years ago, before Stonehenge was begun, and abandoned some 600 years later, just as the great pyramid at Cheops was nearing completion. Skara Brae is not the oldest settlement surviving from Scotland's remote past, but it is by far and away the best-preserved Stone Age village in northern Europe.

Maes Howe, Orkney

Grass-covered Maes Howe, on Mainland Orkney, is quite simply the finest chambered tomb surviving in north-west Europe. Entering it dispels any lingering doubts we might harbour that our remote ancestors were 'noble savages'. Built 5000 years ago, Maes Howe and its neighbouring stone circles of Brodgar and Stenness, together with Skara Brae, today form the Heart of Neolithic Orkney World Heritage Site.

Ketligill Head, Lang Ayre & Turls Head, North Mainland, Shetland

The stretch of coast north from Ketligill Head (foreground) to the distant headland of The Ness and the tiny islet of Uyea is typical of Shetland. Grassy headlands nose into the sea like alligators about to go swimming, whilst between them arc crescent bays, their red-brown shingle floors fringed with white ocean spray. Here and there the odd inlet, or geo, pierces the steep cliffs.

Jarlshof, Shetland

At the end of the nineteenth century, violent storms ripped open the low cliffs at Jarlshof, near the southern tip of Shetland, to reveal an extraordinary settlement site reaching from the late Stone Age over 4000 years ago to the seventeenth century AD. The complex is a maze of walls, but looking down on them from above helps us to understand them better. Bottom right – Stone Age houses dating from before 2500 BC. Bottom centre and left – large round Bronze Age and Iron Age houses built in the first millennium BC. Left – one half of a broch (the rest has disappeared into the sea), built about 100 BC, but subsequently incorporated into a confusing complex of circular 'wheelhouses'. Right – a Viking farm, established around AD 850, centred on the longhouse. Centre left – Jarlshof itself, the 'earl's house', built by Earl Robert Stewart around 1570. The little stones in the courtyard to its right are said to mark the graves of shipwrecked mariners.

St Ninian's Tombolo, Shetland

Four figures stroll across the fine tombolo of sand, heading for St Ninian's Isle. To either side lie the inviting emerald-green waters of St Ninian's Bay (left) and Bigton Wick. The picture is one of utter serenity, but when the Vikings appeared on the scene around AD 800 all was mayhem and bloodshed here. The magnificent hoard of rich silverware buried beneath the floor of St Ninian's Church on the Isle testifies to that.

Mousa Broch, Shetland

Broch towers are unique to Scotland, and Mousa Broch is the best preserved of them all. Its double-skinned walls rise to a height of 43 ft (13 m) and are featureless save for the single low entrance doorway on this west side. Mousa is a powerful reminder of the troubled times that confronted our Iron Age ancestors over 2000 years ago. It was still serving as a defence a thousand years later when Earl Harald of Orkney besieged Moseyarborg, thinking his mother was being held there.

Muckle Flugga & Herma Ness, Unst, Shetland

Here we are, at the end of our long journey, looking back southward from the most northerly point in the British Isles. In the foreground, where the stormy waters of the North Sea and Atlantic Ocean meet, the famous Muckle Flugga lighthouse clings limpet-like to its exposed rocky perch, while beyond the giant turtle that is Herma Ness, stretches the windswept island of Unst. This remote corner of Scotland, on latitude 60°51′, and equidistant from Bergen in Norway, Torshavn in Faroe and Aberdeen, feels like the end of the world. Was this place perhaps what the Romans knew as Ultima Thule, 'the last island'?

We have come a long way since we set out from Edinburgh and the Borders, far to the south. We have soared like an eagle over high mountain peaks and heavy laden cornfields, across sparsely peopled islands and densely packed cities. We have gazed down on megalithic tombs, mighty medieval castles, and monuments from our more recent past. But as we look back south from the most northerly point in Britain, those images seem another world away.

Index of Photographs

First published in Great Britain in 2005 by
Lomond Books
36 West Shore Road,
Granton, Edinburgh EH5 1QD

Produced by Colin Baxter Photography Ltd
Copyright © Colin Baxter Photography Ltd 2005

All photographs copyright © Colin Baxter 2005
except: pages 2, 5, 6, 28, 64, 92, 110, 130, 152, 153
Copyright © PlanetObserver M-SAT www.planetobserver.com

Text by Chris Tabraham,
Copyright © Colin Baxter Photography Ltd 2005

All rights reserved

No part of this book may be reproduced, stored in a
retrieval system or transmitted in any form or by any means
without the prior written permission of the publisher.

A CIP catalogue record for this book is available
from the British Library

ISBN 1-84204-045-6   Printed in China

Front cover photograph: **The Scottish Parliament Building.**   Back cover photographs: **Gleann Einich, Cairngorms** *(top left)*, **Falkirk Wheel** *(bottom left)*,
Glasgow Tenement Buildings *(top right)* and **Iona** *(bottom right)*.   Page 1 photograph: **Barrisdale Bay, Loch Hourn & the Mountains of Lochaber.**

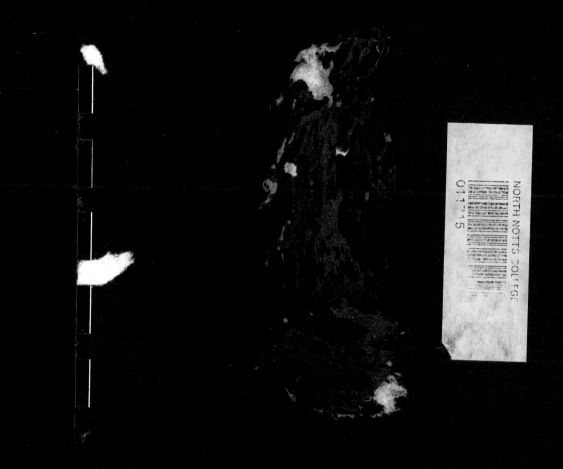

NORTH NOTTS COLLEGE

011715